# WEIRD

**The strangest stories & oddest images from around the world**

# WORLD

First published September 2009

# Bradt

Bradt Travel Guides Ltd
23 High Street, Chalfont St Peter, Bucks SL9 9QE, England
www.bradtguides.com

Published in the USA by The Globe Pequot Press Inc,
246 Goose Lane, PO Box 480, Guilford,
Connecticut 06475-0480

# Wanderlust

Co-published by Wanderlust Publications Ltd
1 Leworth Place, Mellor Walk, Windsor SL4 1EB, UK
www.wanderlust.co.uk, www.gowander.com

Images copyright © 2009 Individual photographers
as credited
Text copyright © 2009 Wanderlust Publications Ltd &
Bradt Travel Guides Ltd, except as credited
Project manager (Bradt): Donald Greig
Project manager (Wanderlust): Paul Bloomfield
Editorial team: Sarah Baxter, Anna Webber,
Sarah Kiernan, Tami Halliday, Ali Webb
Art director: Graham Berridge
Designer: Michelle Rive
Wanderlust Editor-in-Chief: Lyn Hughes

British Library Cataloguing in Publication Data
A catalogue record for this book is available from the
British Library

UK edition ISBN-13: 978 1 84162 318 4
US edition ISBN: 978 1 84162 302 3

Printed and bound in India by Nutech Photolithographers

# Contents

BEWARE
LOW-FLYING
TEAROOMS

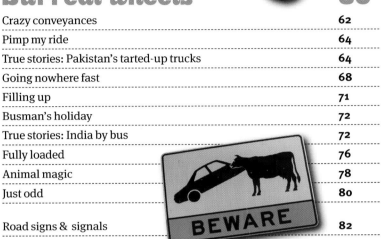

BEWARE
LOW-FLYING
TEAROOMS

NV54 OYZ

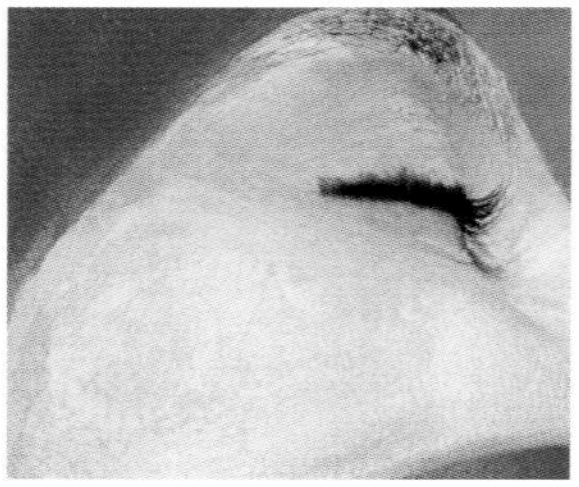
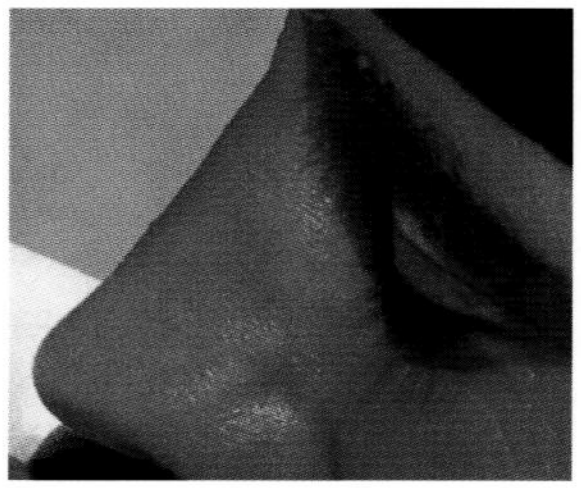
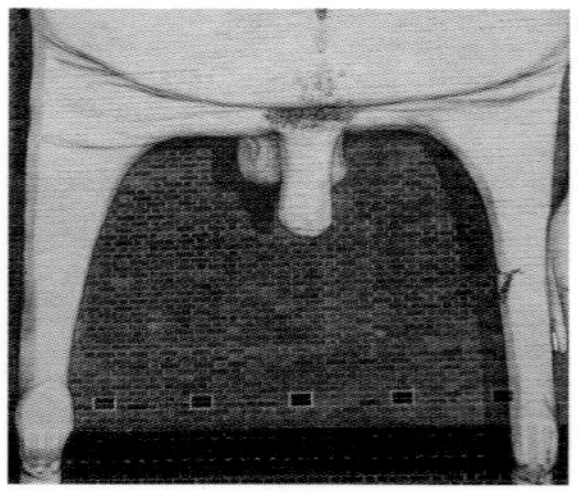

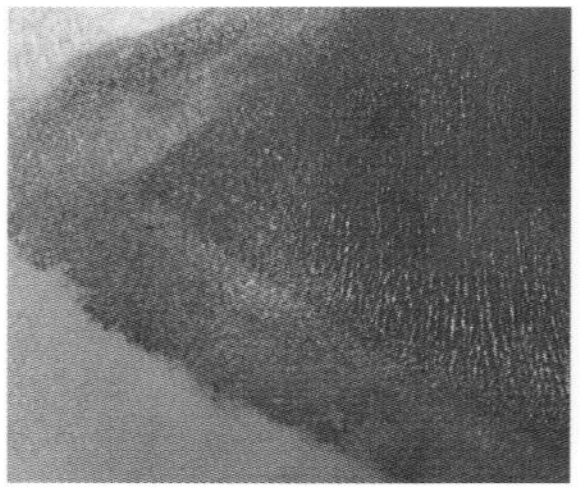
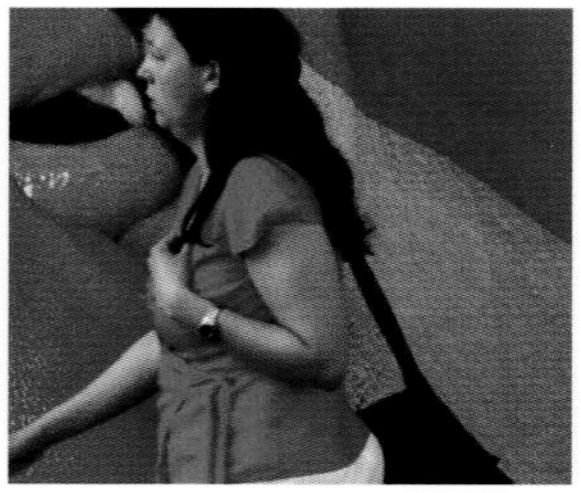

VIAGRA
NATURALE

ON YOUR PLATE
3 km
PRAIRIE HOTEL
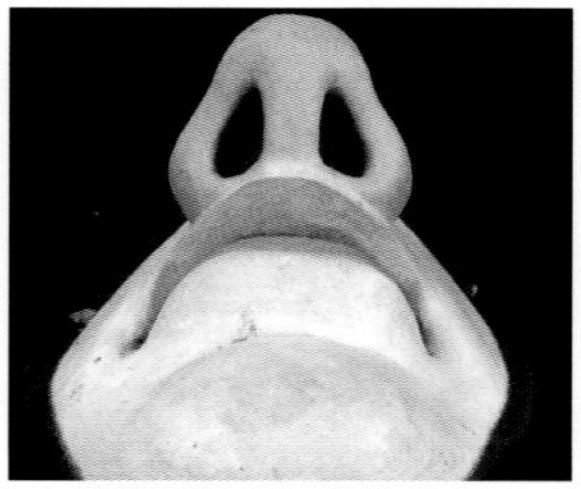

# Welcome to our
## WEIRD WORLD

If there's one image in these pages that really captures what the whole book is about, it's on page 17. The photographer described the moment: "At the same time as someone out on the deep Playa set off several enormous black smoke rings ... a shiny blue alien cycled by."

Anywhere else in the world, the sight would be a newsworthy event; at Nevada's Burning Man Festival, nobody raised an eyebrow. It's all about context.

Travellers travel in order to experience the novel, and they're rarely disappointed. Something that's considered a dangerous pest in one country is a tasty treat in another. It might be illegal in Kansas, but spiritual in Kuala Lumpur; newsworthy in Brisbane, not worth a glance in Bolivia.

It's that diversity of experiences that keeps us excited about exploring the world: we never know what's around the next corner – but we do know it'll probably make us laugh (or, quite possibly, run for cover). The people who contributed the photos and stories that populate this book are just like us – and you. We're celebrating and documenting the unusual, in the hope of inspiring more explorers to set out to discover new horizons.

Join us on a journey across our weird world. And expect the unexpected.

# People are strange

It's the differences that make meeting people around the world so fascinating – and these characters are truly different…

**Extreme acupuncture:** "The Phuket Vegetarian Festival is one of the weirdest on the planet. Devotees go into trances and take on the spirits of the local deities, then perform macabre acts of self-mutilation while walking through the town and blessing everyone for the coming year."
*Dave Stamboulis*

# 6,785,609,620 reasons to be weird

**T**hat, according to the US Census Bureau World Population Clock, was the estimated (human) population of the world at the time this page was sent to print. By the time it hit the bookshops two months later, that would already have increased by around 13 million – the rate of growth of the global population is astonishing. Depending on who you ask, those 6.8 billion people live in 195 different countries, follow more than 4,200 religions and speak some 6,700 languages – so with such incomprehensible diversity, it's no wonder people do things that seem odd to outsiders. We're simply all that different.

But then some things are just odd.

Wherever you are – in a traditional Beijing hutong, or on Oxford Street – seeing a naked man hurtling down a busy street *(right)* would seem weird. Sticking a chair through your face? A bit weird. Coating yourself in concrete and sitting in an armchair on a bustling square? Plain nuts.

People photography isn't always easy. Even when they're acting weird, people often act, well, weirder when you try to take a photo. So this collection of snaps is even more remarkable for the fact that our photographers managed to capture these moments and escape with camera (and nose) intact.

Often the characters encapsulated in these pages are performing, in one way or another – to crowds, to each other, to themselves – and the costumes and disguises they don add to the sense of being out of kilter with the familiar world. Then again, some people express themselves by wearing less – *much* less – rather than more. In the right places, that's a show of reverence or self-expression; in other situations, freedom. At the South Pole? Lunacy.

We're not judging. We're not even sniggering (well, maybe just a little). No: this is a celebration of diversity – of the costumes, the festivals, the traditions, the beliefs, the interactions and the reactions. It's human behaviour at its most fascinating.

**Right:** Beijing's *hutong* (labyrinthine alleys) are the last bastions of traditional life in the Chinese capital. Understandable, then, that "This was quite a shock to see" for the photographer. *Steve Morgan*

# Eccentric events

## WHAT TO LOOK FOR WHERE ON YOUR GLOBAL TRAVELS

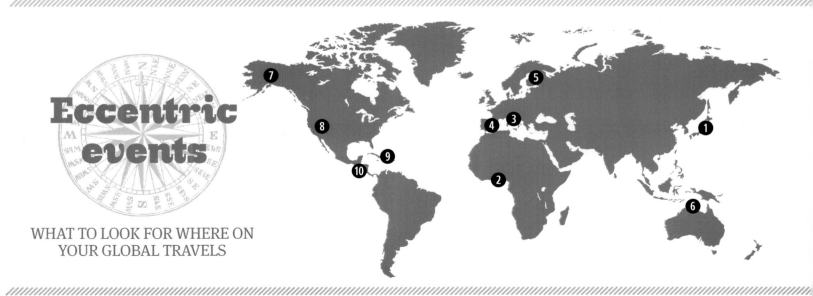

## WEIRD WEDDINGS

➜ In 1976 a Los Angeles secretary called Jannene Swift married a 20kg rock

➜ A German woman called Eija-Riitta Berliner-Mauer wed the Berlin Wall in 1979

➜ In Bangladesh in March 2009 two frogs were married in a lavish ceremony to end a drought

❶ **Hadaka Matsuri (Naked Festival), Japan (January)** Watch Japanese men strip to their smalls, roll in ice and jump in cold water for extreme purification – most manic in Inazawa.

❷ **Voodoo Festival, Ouidah, Benin (January)** The high priest kicks off with the slaughter of a goat before chanting, dancing and gin-drinking aplenty takes over.

❸ **Festival of the Snakes, Cocullo, Italy (May)** Ophidiophobics beware: in this Abruzzan town, St Domenic is venerated with snakes – lots of them – slithering around his statue.

❹ **El Colacho (Baby-jumping Festival), Castrillo de Murcia, near Burgos, Spain (May/June)** Would you let a whip-wielding devil hurdle your newborn? In Castilla y León the parents queue up for it, believing it purges their little'uns of evil.

❺ **Wife Carrying World Championships, Sonkajärvi, Finland (July)** Men lug their wives over 250m of obstacles for the ultimate prize – their wife's weight in beer.

❻ **Beer Can Regatta, Darwin, Australia (July)** In true Aussie style, this does exactly what it says on the tinnie: drink beer; create boat from resultant cans; paddle it until it sinks; drink more beer. Bonza!

❼ **Moose Dropping Festival, Talkeetna, Alaska (July)** A tonne of numbered turds is dumped onto a bullseye – if your dropping is closest, the prize is yours. Classy.

❽ **Burning Man, Nevada, USA (Aug/Sep)** Anything goes in the 40°C heat of the Nevada Desert – naked parades, out-there art, fire-breathing street performers and a hippy ethos take over an ancient lake bed.

❾ **Fête Gede, Port-au-Prince, Haiti (November)** Voodoo shenanigans on the Caribbean island: locals flock to cemeteries to honour the dead with flowers and rum.

❿ **Feast of St Thomas, Chichicastenango, Guatemala (December)** Fireworks, parades and daredevils unravelling on ropes from 30m-high poles – Central America's most high-octane fiesta?

# )Festival fever

## Thailand's Vegetarian Festival

At the start of the ninth lunar month (October/November), Phuket's Chinese community abstains from meat – and proceeds to thrust large objects through their faces...

"**A** young man appeared. He was sweating, though the tropical sun had not yet risen above the roof line. He seemed relaxed, though with an unshakable level of concentration. He wore a decorated red tunic, but otherwise looked unremarkable.

Except, that is, for the metallic pole passing straight through his cheeks.

He was just the first in a long procession. There were men with multiple blades skewered through each side of their faces and limbs pierced with dozens of needles. Many seemed to have entered a 'stick the most unusual and unexpected implement through your face' competition – hedge clippers, vegetation, musical instruments, rifles and umbrellas were among the more identifiable examples.

One of the more bloody acts of self-mortification involved a devotee carrying a saw blade, which he licked in a vigorous fashion, drawing trickles of salivated blood from his mouth. At one stage men sporting large curved blades stopped nearby and, upon a spontaneous, unified, guttural call, flagellated themselves, drawing streams of blood down their own backs. Amazingly, a calm and peaceful atmosphere pervaded the entire proceedings.

It was beguiling: an unabashed expression of human devotion and camaraderie, which accentuated our untapped reservoirs of spiritual and physical potential. As the sun crept steadfastly upwards throughout the day I felt that I'd also been drawn into a trance-like state, induced by the incredible sights and communal good will all around."
*Johnny Lawlor*

 **"They seemed to have entered a 'stick the most unexpected implement through your face' competition"**

**Cheek thrills:** As well as facial piercing and fire-walking, parades and firework displays liven up Phuket's Vegetarian Festival. *Photos: Dave Stamboulis (top); Johnny Lawlor (above, opposite)*

**Right, opposite top right, top far right & below left:** "Thaipusam festival at the Batu Caves outside Kuala Lumpur, Malaysia."
*Johnny Lawlor*

**Opposite, below centre & far right:** "These two pictures were taken in Sri Srinivas Peramul Temple in Serangoon Road, Singapore, during the Thaipusam festival in February. Thaipusam is a Hindu festival; the piercing has been largely banned in India for being, well, a little freaky, but is practiced in Singapore, Malaysia and Mauritius. Devotees give thanks to the Lord Murugan by carrying a 'Kavadi', or burden, on a 4km parade. The Kavadi can be as simple as a milk pot or can involve numerous piercings of the face and body. The first chap is also hanging limes off his chest on fish hooks; the second chap has had his tongue pierced to prevent him from speaking, in order to receive the thoughts of Lord Murugan."
*Anthony White*

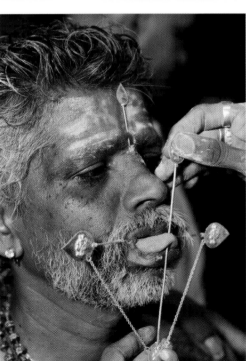

**Far left, top:** Holi is the Hindu festival of colours, celebrated in India and Nepal. If you're around during the festival wear old clothes – paint-flinging is a matter of course!"
*Raphael Pilot*

**Far left, below:** "This woman is taking part in a fire-walking festival in honour of the goddess Drowpthy Amman in Bangalore, India. The festival lasts 40 days, with one evening of firewalking. Most participants show no pain. 'If you pray, you will be protected,' I was told, when trying to understand how the participants walk on hot ash."
*Stuart Forster*

**Left:** "To honour Guru Rinopche, Bhutanese monks don masks and dance at the *tsechu*, a religious festival held annually in each district. Dressed as wrathful deities, the monks embody the spirits that people will encounter after death to alleviate their fears about the afterlife."
*Kim Walker*

**This page:** "At the same time as someone out on the deep Playa set off several enormous black smoke rings, our next-door neighbour rode by dressed as a shiny blue alien. Just your average day at Burning Man Festival, Nevada, USA."
*Sonia Zamborsky*

# }Costume dramas

**Far left:** "Every Sunday in Harajuku, Tokyo, there's a massive gathering of bizarrely dressed and made-up people, many of them teenagers. Some dress as punks, some as Little Bo Peep, some in wedding dresses. This girl struck me – she'd gone to such an effort that she'd even got a red contact lens to match her outfit and hair."
*Sophie Atkinson*

**Left:** "Is is a statue? No, it's a man painted in gold who pretends to be a statue and moves whenever someone gives him money"
*Marilyn Champagne*

**Below left:** "Some people like role-playing games. And some take it a little more seriously than others…"
*Graham Berridge*

**Right:** "Halloween in New York City: this woman is getting made up for the occasion, using the car wing mirror to transform herself from semi-naked women to painted lady."
*Laura Watts*

**Left:** "I found the 'concrete man' on Plaza Mayor in Madrid."
*Paul Biseth*

**Right:** "I was fortunate enough to be in Uyuni, Bolivia, when they were holding an annual festival – Fraternidad Bambinos – during which groups dressed up in different costumes and marched through the town, singing and throwing flour, eggs and water at each other. These groups were dressed as Batman and Superman. I watched from the comfort of my hotel room's balcony above the main crossing."
*Sophie Atkinson*

**Far right, top:** "This lady was in a Tamberma village in northern Togo. I have no idea of the significance of her horned helmet – it could be just something put on for tourists to take photos of!"
*Rhoda Allen*

**Below right:** "Che on the mind – or certainly on this guy's head. I spotted him at Havana Airport, Cuba."
*Kiki Streitberger*

**Far right, below:** "For three nights we stayed in a small village close to Bwindi Impenetrable Forest National Park, Uganda. The night before we went in search of gorillas, the local children came to dance as a symbol of good luck and safe passage into the forest."
*Andrew White*

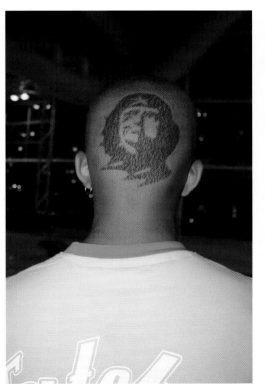

# }Bizarre behaviour

**Above:** "This guy is taking his pig for a walk along the streets of Trinidad, Cuba." Of course he is...
*Paul Biseth*

**Right:** "It's a wombat on a lead going for a walk – not much more to say, really! I took this at Australia Zoo, Queensland, Australia."
*Chris Hopkinson*

**Top right:** "On a day trip to Cape Point from Cape Town, South Africa, I was accompanied by Catfish – self-proclaimed World Champion, Working Man and World Traveller. He wore a hat boasting of his travel accolades and his love of World Travel – yet hardly spoke to anyone the whole day!"
*Sophie Atkinson*

**Far right:** Morning exercises on Shanghai's Bund are... unique!
*Paul Morrison*

# TRUE STORIES: stripping off at the South Pole

"Visiting the South Pole is a strange experience in itself, but what I saw there left me shaking my head in disbelief. I'd heard about the 300 Club – to become a member you have to rush out from a 200°F (93°C) sauna to -100°F (-73°C) temperatures outside, wearing only footwear – so I knew that stripping off at the South Pole wasn't a totally unusual occurrence. But the tourists don't usually do it. And certainly not like this.

After a brief tour of the Amundsen-Scott South Pole Station, we wandered around outside, the temperature a balmy -30°C (-50°C with wind-chill). We took pictures of frozen eyelashes, the little pole-marker, the sign bearing the heartbreaking quote from Scott ('The Pole. Yes, but under very different circumstances from those expected') and then, finally, the array of flags.

At this point, one of the group – a middle-aged American computer programmer – decided to strip down to his long boxer shorts, with his layers of trousers gathered around his knees. After a few frozen batteries and eventual photos he hurriedly dressed again. But as we were walking off another man decided to join him – a retired Japanese diplomat (*above*) – "for honour".

Nothing prepared me for the sight when he removed his last layers: a tiny black lacy G-string modestly covering his shrivelled bits. He stood in a hero pose with a huge grin on his face, while I took pictures and the station manager tried to recover from the shock of the bizarre spectacle. It took a good five minutes for us both to stop laughing.

I look back at the photos of my extravagant trip with nostalgia, but the memory of the Japanese man in his lady's knickers makes me giggle."
*Sophie Atkinson*

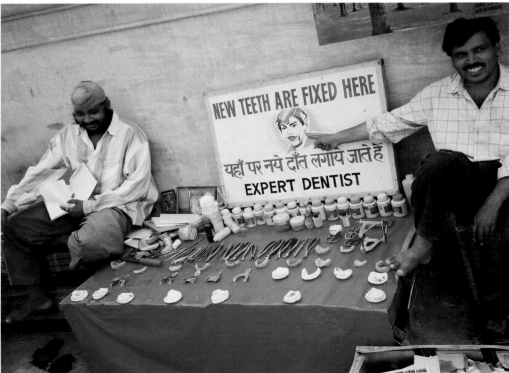

## TRUE STORIES: battered in Bolivia

"Bolivian female wrestling was just becoming popular in 90s La Paz, and one night Dave and I stumbled on a ramshackle downtown gym on fight night. Barely standing after too much pisco, we were the only two gringos there and, when the announcer called for volunteers to fight one round with 'Condor Rosa', Dave – naturally – nominated me.

Condor Rosa was 5'1" to my 6'3", 7 stone to my 16. I was 26, a karate black belt and a champion kick-boxer. She was 47, an Aymara mother-of-six in full traditional dress – two long black pigtails under a bowler hat and oceans of coloured petticoats, with an over-cape of black (presumably condor) feathers. I smiled to say "Don't worry!" – and she punched me squarely in the throat, jabbed both thumbs in my eyes, then stamped hard on my instep and head-butted me flush on the chin.

As I went down, half-blind and gagging, she slammed an elbow across my cheekbone. Then she started climbing the ropes for a full-on body slam.

I rolled out of range and staggered up. I was nearly vomiting, had blurred vision, my head was ringing, and my tongue bitten through and bloody. Condor Rosa climbed off the ropes and, without thinking, on pure instinct, I threw a hard left and right: bang, BANG!

Her eyes rolled up to the whites, her bowler hat flew over the top rope and she hit the canvas spread-eagled in a perfect crucifix.

There was total silence in the room for about ten seconds. Then someone threw a bottle (*Ay! Ay! Ay!*), and Dave shouted, "Time to go!"

I'm still mortified about it, and I sincerely hope that the wonderful Condor Rosa picked herself up and is still body-slamming today."
*Sergeant_Pluck, on www.goWander.com*

**Clockwise from left:** "Sunday afternoon wrestling in La Paz is staged in a dilapidated sports hall with regular power cuts and some less-than-athletic-looking wrestlers. The highlight is undoubtedly the female wrestlers – this one not faring too well, having been thrown out of the ring by an Elvis impersonator."
*Michael Hylton*

"An expert dentist in India."
*Juraj Kaman*

"In Hanoi, Vietnam, barbers work along the streets, covering the pavement with black snow. The reflection of the man's expression transcends any language barrier: I think we can all relate to being unconvinced by a hairdresser's work. But it looks OK from the back…"
*Philomena Thomas*

"I met this man in Karimabad in Pakistan. His moustaches were amazing – I particularly loved the way he'd tuck the ends behind his ears!"
*Sarah Baxter*

"Another Indian dentist – an outdoor stomatology surgery in Jammu and Kashmir. You'll notice that dentistry isn't the only specialisation of this doctor – he's also an optician!"
*Juraj Kaman*

# }Signs: lost in translation

## The music Room
### (Chinese name:Qing-Shi)

This Pavilion/room is a Place for playing a certain musical instrument, something like the Japancse, in the past. The environment is quite. There are a music desk and music brick there. In front of the pavilion, there are a potteed pomegranate, a half-precipice rockery and an Chinese date and bamboo groves. The scenery is very plain, simple, but attractive, and very suitable for the tourist.

旅游咨询电话 65203131
Travel to consult telephone

旅游投诉电话 65223377
Traveling the hurl tells the telephone

TECHNICAL TESTING COMMITTEE BRANCH.
VEHICLES TESTING.
TAXI DRIVERS TESTING.
RENTING OFFICE.

فرع لجان الفحص الفنية
فحص الآليات
فحص سائقي الاجرة
مكتب التاجير

## WARNING !
DEAR DRIVERS,HOPE YOU TO KEEP ROADS CLEAN,NO SPIT OR THROW DOWN GARBAGES FROM CAR WINDOW WHILE DRIVING OR STOPPING. PLEASE FLING IT IN PROPER PLACES TO BE EXAMPLE FOR OTHERS.
IF NOT OBEY THESE INSTRUCTIONS,AUTHORITIES SHOULD BE FORCED TO DRAW YOUR DRIVING LICENCE.

古建修缮施工，给
您带来了不便请您谅解.
The ancient building is renovating
Excuse me for bringing trouble to you.

# 疯狂说英语
## Crazily Speak English

李阳 主编/主讲

- I'm sure you'll enjoy it.
- What do you recommend?
- That's impressive.
- Are you sure you can make it?
- How long have you been learning English?
- Let me know if you change your mind.
- I know you'll be able to take care of it.
- Can you help me with my English?
- In my opinion, Chinese people are very friendly.
- Are you satisfied with my work?

花旗帝国

SHAMPOO·GROUP·NEW
BEAT THE EYE·HOLE·CASE!

SKIN THE FACES.

### Ferg Rules

Must sign the quantity of passengers and goods that a boat can be allowed to carrg at the most at the obvious places of the boats and the ferries Don't allow any boat with overloading .

In order to avoid accident passengers ougat to obey the ferry rules protect the ferry arrangments and wack into the boat with turs then listen to the crew

Forbid any boat to set out if there is flood heavy windy or another badly weather .

Don't set saie for the boats that are broken or have no complete driving instruments .

keep the deformed sick and drunk crew off drivi ne boat

Everyone has responsibility to see each other and obey them for your safety .

VOYAGE MANAGEMENT OFFICE OF LESHAN BUDDHA 'RE-GION FERRY

MANAGEMENT OFFICE OF LESHAN CITY

## WELCOME TO CAT BA PLAZA HOTEL

TEL : 031.888129   FAX : 031.887729

### PLAZA RESTAURANT
*Special Europe and Asia Foods*

- * MINI BAR - KARAOKE
- * BILLARDS - SNOOKER
- * BUS ( 15 - 45 SEATS ) TO NATIONAL PARK,TRUNG TRANG CAVE
- * MOTORS AND BICYCLES FOR RENT
- * BOAT AND CANOE TO SEE LAN HA BAY CAT DUA ISLAND VIET HAI VILLAGE
- * EXPRESS BOATTICKET
- * KAYAKS FOR RENT

*Happy to sever You!*

## 便民服务
## Free Services

1、免费使用雨伞
Free use of umbrellas

2、免费使用轮椅车
Free use of wheelchair

3、免费使用婴儿车
Free use of baby carriage

4、免费使用拐杖
Free use of cane

5、免费使用针线包
Free use of sewing kits

Chris Prior; Chris Chacksfield; David Williams; Timothy Bird; Shelly Stetsko; Marilyn Willwohl; Glenn Winch; Marieke Verbruggen

# A taste for the unusual

From camel balls to bottled snakes, the cuisine of some countries takes experimental eating to new levels. Strong stomach required...

**A shade unusual:** "This splendidly myopic specimen was seen in a butcher's shop in the Italian hilltop village of Pitigliano, Tuscany, advertising the regional speciality of wild boar."
*Lesley Heptinstall*

# Would YOU eat a SPIDER?

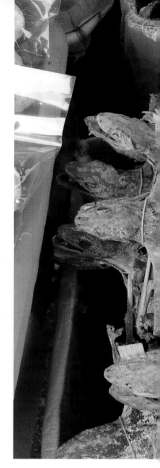

You say potato, I say potato. I say guinea pig, you say 'a tasty treat, deep-fried whole, teeth and all, best dished up with chips'.

In today's era of multinational business and pan-global media, we're all exposed to many of the same brands and influences. But while it's hard to escape the reaches of Coke, McDonald's or Starbucks however far you travel, certain ingestive habits haven't been shared across the planet quite so enthusiastically. Let's face it: most of us are a little bit squeamish, if we're honest – crunchy spiders are extremely unlikely to be the next culinary craze sweeping Europe or the United States.

But why? After all, tucking into a prawn, lobster or ring of calamari seems perfectly normal – it's not as if we have a problem with munching things with shells, spidery legs or tentacles. But then people aren't always fortunate enough to be able to choose what they eat; in Cambodia, the habit of snacking on spiders developed during the famine years of the Khmer Rouge. If spiders are all you can find to eat in order to survive, squeamishness is soon sacrificed.

Perhaps it's conditioning. At a young age we learn what things are food and which aren't, which is why in England, for example, rabbit goes in the pot while guinea pigs stay out of the oven, and why cows face a less certain future than horses (which, in some other European countries, are as likely to be roasted as ridden).

Being able to recognise your food plays a big part; the meat sold in Western butchers is usually pre-cut into anonymous, inoffensive lumps; head for a camel butcher's shop in any Arabic country from Morocco to Iran and you'll be left in no doubt as to what you're buying.

At the end of the day, it's a matter of taste. Which is something that's a lot stronger if your food's been buried for several months to ferment (like Icelandic shark *hákarl*) or, as in the case of Sardinian cheese *casu marzu*, comes served still infested with live-and-wriggling maggots. Yum!

**Right:** "These dried out, flattened and clearly very dead lizards (bless their souls) in Vancouver's Chinatown are meant to be a fertility aid – though how you use them, I don't know..."
*Andrea Wren*

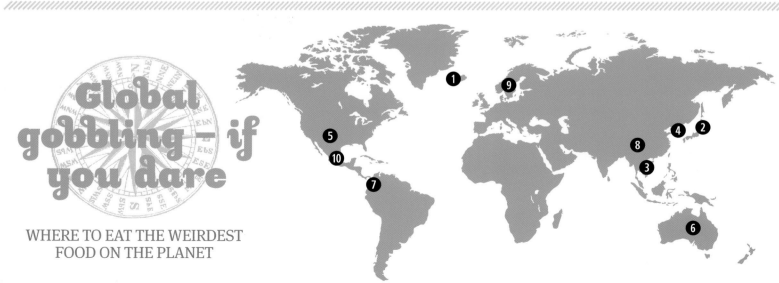

## Global gobbling – if you dare

WHERE TO EAT THE WEIRDEST FOOD ON THE PLANET

## FREAKY FOOD FACTS

➤ Following Popeye's creation in 1931, spinach consumption in the USA went up by 33%

➤ Kopi luwak coffee is made from berries that have been part-digested by an Asian civet

➤ The Burnt Food Museum in Arlington, Massachusetts, was closed – due to fire damage

**❶ Fermented shark, Iceland** With a whiff like fishy bleach, the biggest battle with consuming fermented shark (*hákarl*) – which is first buried for up to 12 weeks, then hung for several months – is being able to stomach the smell.

**❷ Puffer fish, Japan** The food that fights back – Japanese puffer fish (*fugu*) is deadly if prepared incorrectly, first paralysing then asphyxiating the diner. Still hungry?

**❸ Duck embryo, South-East Asia** *Balut* – fertilised duck or chicken egg containing a nearly developed embryo – is boiled and eaten in the shell. Enough said.

**❹ Sea slugs, Korea** Pulled live from a tank, then sliced and gutted before your eyes, this is not a dish for the slime-averse.

**❺ Prairie oysters, USA** Known euphemistically as *huevos del toro* (literally, 'bull's eggs') and 'cowboy caviar', there's no escaping what these actually are – the peeled and peppered testicles of an unfortunately emasculated bull.

**❻ Witchetty grubs, Australia** A popular Aboriginal snack, this pale and chubby bug should be extracted from the roots of the witchetty tree then consumed immediately – live and wriggling.

**❼ Roasted ants, Colombia** The perfect high-protein, low-fat snack? South America's *Atta laevigata* ants, called *bachaco*, have been harvested, de-winged, roasted and eaten for centuries.

**❽ Fish maw, China** Yellow and puffy, with a texture like sponge, these fish flotation bladders are a popular – and surprisingly pricey – addition to many soups.

**❾ Fermented herring, Sweden** *Surströmming* unleashes an odour of pure evil when its tin is opened – even the strong-nosed Swedes generally eat it outside.

**❿ Grasshoppers, Mexico** Eaten by peckish locals for more than 3,000 years, toasted grasshoppers (*chapulines*) have a singular taste. Just try not to get the legs stuck in your teeth.

# }Ugh!

## GOURMET GUINEA PIGS: don't be cuy

**W**hether it's the rigid pose and grin-grimace facial expression or the memories of your squeaking childhood pet, there's something extremely disturbing about a plateful of barbecued guinea pig.

Served up across Peru, Ecuador and Bolivia, *cuy* has long been a staple dish of indigenous Andeans, its small proportions making it easier to rear than traditional livestock. But its popularity now extends beyond the highlands; in Peru, in particular, it's ingrained in the national psyche. In Cuzco's main cathedral, cuy is even laid before Christ and his disciples in a painting of the Last Supper.

Travellers will encounter guinea pig in many forms: from the live bundles of fluff snuffling around traditional village homes to the *asado* (broiled), *frito* (fried) and *al horno* (roasted) versions squealing from many a restaurant menu.

It's not so much a gastronomic sensation – guess what? It tastes like chicken – or a feast for the hungry (there's not a lot of meat on these little blighters). No, it's more a culinary challenge: can you face a ruby-red, splayed-limbed, former cute-and-cuddly (with chips) staring up from your dinner plate?

### How to cook fried guinea pig (Ayacucho style)

**INGREDIENTS**

1 guinea pig – de-haired, gutted and cleaned

½ cup flour

½ teaspoon ground cumin

Salt & black pepper

½ cup oil

**METHOD**

1 Dry the prepared guinea pig. Rub with the cumin, salt and pepper.
2 Preheat the oil.
3 Dust the carcass with the flour and place it on its back in the oil, turning frequently to cook both sides. (You could chop it into quarters, but then it won't look so frightening on a plate.)
4 Serve with boiled manioc root or potatoes and a salad of tomatoes and onions bathed in lime juice and salt. You may also want a beer. Or four.

Opposite: "We picked up this book on breeding and rearing guinea pigs in central Peru; there's a tasty-looking recipe section at the very end."
*Kris Weber*

## "In Cuzco cathedral, guinea pig is served to Christ and his disciples in a painting of the Last Supper"

Above: "There's just something about the way it looks on the plate..."
*Philip Darbyshire*

Far left: "This one still had its teeth attached – made me feel quite ill!"
*Claire Sharp*

Left: "My first ever guinea pig – eaten near Huaraz, Peru. Although it tasted pretty good, the remains – claws, head, snout – didn't make for a pretty sight. It just highlights how a national dish in one nation is met with disgust in another."
*Gregory Froome*

# )Just a nip

**Above:** "Snakes in bottles at an airport shop in Hanoi, Vietnam. I wondered how one would get them through customs in Britain; I didn't attempt it!"
*Sophie Collard*

**Above right:** "This drink is sold in many countries in Asia, such as Laos and Vietnam. This photo was taken in 'snake village', Hanoi, where you also can order 'snake à la carte'."
*Julia Lövenich*

**Right:** "After a long day of exploring the deserted streets of Saigon (Ho Chi Minh City) the day after Chinese New Year and not finding any excitement, why not head to the only open pub to see what there is to drink? Wine? Whisky? How about a strange concoction of rum, peppers, scorpion and cobra? Perfect!"
*Josh Flannigan*

**Opposite:** "Mother-in-law's ruin – that's what the vendor in Luang Prabang, Laos, described it as!"
*Mick Walton*

# 10 RUM REMEDIES

**❶ Vuka-vuka, Zimbabwe** The secret ingredient of 'African Viagra' is extract of *Myalabris* beetle – guaranteed to reach parts other beetles can't.

**❷ Dry peas, Japan** Reputed to be very useful for driving away evil spirits.

**❸ Dried penis, Sicily** Boozy night? No problem! Just munch on the dehydrated appendage of an emasculated bull for hangover relief. Simple...

**❹ Pins, Haiti** ...Or do as the voodoo with a hangover – stick 13 pins in the cork of the offending bottle to take away the pain.

**❺ Shoe-smelling, India** As a response to a fit, passers-by may attempt to bring the sole of the afflicted's shoe under their nose – strong whiffs can allegedly halt seizures.

**❻ Kimchi, South Korea** Sales of the potent fermented cabbage dish went through the roof when scientists suggested it could help cure bird flu (but not bad breath).

**❼ Chillis, Mexico** Good for everything, from blocked noses to sore throats to constipation. Sprinkle chilli powder on your socks and mittens to ward off chills.

**❽ Toothbrush tree, Sudan** Chew on the wood of the *Salvadora persica* (toothbrush tree) to release an anti-bacterial sap that fights decay.

**❾ Didgeridoo playing, Australia** No, really: scientists have found that blowing this Aboriginal instrument exercises the tissues in the throat, thus helping to prevent sleep apnoea.

**❿ Dragon's blood, Yemen** This tree resin is another cure-all (treating diarrhoea, dysentery, ulcers, fevers...); it also makes spells more potent.

**Opposite:** "There are *escargots* the French way – and then there are snails the Peruvian way. One of these monsters, on sale in Belem market, would be enough for a whole meal."
*Anne Frigon*

**Top:** "I spotted this outside a greengrocer's shop in Amalfi, Italy. Definitely one for the boys!"
*Bobbie Russell*

**Above, right:** "These herbs, found in northern Thailand, looked just like pieces of wood – in fact they're aphrodisiacs and remedies for rheumatism and stomach ailments."
*Peter Karry*

**Right:** "Viagra Touareg: boil those roots, drink the result and you're back in the game. No need for the little blue pills!"
*Kiki Streitberger*

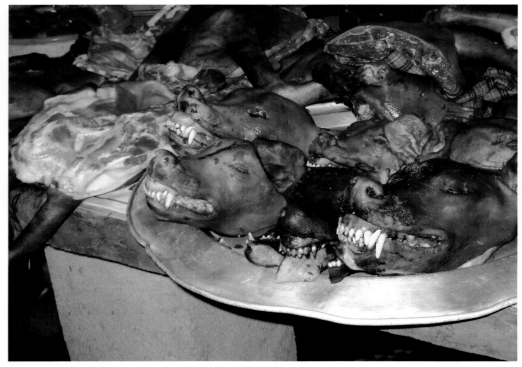

**Top left & right:** "In the fetish market, Togo – these are vital ingredients in various potions that do all manner of miraculous things."
*Rhoda Allen*

**Above:** "Chicken in the central market, Hanoi. Having wandered many markets in Asia, I thought there was little left to shock me. But somehow this did. Maybe it's the elegant pose on the bowl – or perhaps that suspended expression. It's almost like it was stopped mid-sentence…"
*Marika Chalkiadis*

**Left:** "Dogs' heads in a Vietnamese market."
*Isabella & Tanja*

**Above:** "Among the Panama hats and textiles, the butchers' section of Saquisilí market in the highlands of Ecuador had a smiling surprise for us..."
*Pete Browning*

# }Meet your meat

You can't buy camel meat from any old butcher, though those that do sell it are pretty easy to spot: just look for the dromedary-silhouette sign above the door – or the droopy-lipped camel head hanging from the wall.

Once you've located your specialist meat-seller, you need to select your cut. Fat slabs of camel steak (which allegedly taste like superior beef), stew-sized chunks or ground mince balls – ideal for camel kofta – are all available. The cholesterolly unaware can also purchase mounds of hump fat – it's purported to have medicinal benefits.

If none of this appeals, perhaps consider the traditional Bedouin approach: slaughter and skin one whole camel (medium); stuff it with a lamb, 20 chickens, 60 eggs, 12kg of rice and a selection of nuts and spices. Cook the lot over a charcoal pit until brown and crispy, then dish up. Serves 80-100.

**Opposite:** "A special treat at this butcher's stall in Fès, Morocco – anyone for camel head for dinner?"
*Claire Elphick*

**Above:** "Camel meat hanging outside a butcher's shop in Shiraz, Iran."
*Donal O'Leary*

# }Bugs

## Cambodian arach snack attack

**C**ulinary hell? Or arachnophobe's revenge? For many Cambodians, the habit of munching deep-fried *a-ping* (tarantula) developed simply as a method of survival – during the bleak years of the reign of the Khmer Rouge millions of starving people would eat anything to stay alive. The residents of Skuon – dubbed 'Spiderville' – obviously developed a taste for eight-legged lunches that lasted far longer than Pol Pot's brutal regime. This blink-and-you'd-miss-it town, 90km north of Phnom Penh, continues to serve up towering trays of crispy arachnids to passing truckers and bus-loads of curious and (usually) squeamish tourists.

Spider hunters dig up the creepy-crawlies or prise them out of holes with sticks. After a sprinkling of salt, sugar and MSG, they're plunged into hot, garlic-infused oil until the legs are crunchy and the abdomen well cooked.

> ## "If you can get over the hairy legs, enormous proportions and brown gunk inside, they don't taste too bad"

If you can get over the indisputably spidery appearance (there's no attempt to hide the grim truth under a fancy *coulis* here), the hairy legs, the enormous proportions and the unidentifiable brown gunk (eggs? entrails? excrement?) in the middle, they don't taste too bad – unsurprisingly, a little like chicken. They also provide an excellent source of income for the town – both hunters and 'spiderwomen', the giggling ladies doing the selling, make well over the average wage from the tarantula trade.

The culinary legacy of Pol Pot's regime stretches beyond spider snacks, though, as the photos on these pages demonstrate – all kinds of crunchy, charred beasts and bugs are on the menu.

And when you snack on those spiders, just remember: where there's smoke there's fire; and where there are fried spiders on the menu, there are live ones scurrying somewhere nearby, plotting *their* revenge...

**Sequence left:** "Mmmm... tastes like chicken! From raw ingredient to snack as served – and eaten."
*Mick Walton*

**Right, top:** "Deep fried/roasted insects for sale at a roadside market in Siem Reap, Cambodia."
*Garry Ho*

**Far right, top:** "Between Siem Reap and Phnom Penh the bus stops for a break off the dusty, bumpy road for passengers to get a snack. Aside from the random assortment of deep-fried roaches and tarantulas, you can also try charred bird in this corner of Cambodia."
*Josh Flannigan*

**Right, below:** "Spider saleswoman in Skuon, Cambodia – anyone for some yummy, crunchy spider snacks soaked in onion sauce?"
*James Welch*

**Far right, below:** "Bee larvae in 'black chicken soup', served at the Grand Hotel, Taipei, Taiwan."
*Maren Hills*

**Top left:** "Mobile cart selling deep-fried bugs on Khao San Road, Bangkok, Thailand."
*Samantha Dobson*

**Top right:** "Scorpions, crickets and silkworm grubs for sale on one of the food stands on Wangfujing Street in Beijing. The variety of bugs for sale as food was unbelievable. I'm not sure what's more astounding – our astonishment at seeing all these unique foods or the salesman's nonchalant response: 'Really? You don't eat them?'"
*Katy Yu*

**Above left:** "Grubs being sautéed at Inle Lake, Burma."
*Jim Pratt*

**Above right:** "Anyone up for some fresh roasted maggots with their banana daquiri?"
*James Welch*

**Opposite:** "I've heard of fighting for your food, but these snacks in Beijing would have won any day – they were still moving!"
*Anna Spysz*

# Odd eateries

**Far left & left:** "We came across this unusual McDonald's while travelling from Rotorua to Wanganui, New Zealand."
*Derrick Griffin*

**Left, centre:** "Possum, wallaby, emu – as they say at the Roadkill Café: you kill it, we grill it!"
*Andrew Swaffer*

**Far left, below:** "In Cuzco, Peru, we stumbled across a quirky restaurant called the Fallen Angel. Once inside we were sat at our 'table' – a bathtub filled with various fish, covered with a glass top – from which we ate. I can safely say I've never eaten from a bathtub before, and it was wonderful – you could watch the fish swimming under your dinner (presumably thankful they weren't on the menu!)."
*Samantha Evans*

**Left, below:** "The Tourist Burger restaurant is on Imam Square in Isfahan, Iran. Are they really going to eat the tourists? In a bun??"
*Chris Beggs*

**Right:** "I can't remember exactly where in New Zealand this was, but I do remember a long, boring day of just driving. Ready to start banging my head against the steering wheel in boredom, a café in the form of a disused cargo plane popped up around the corner: random, but the highlight of the day. Where else can you have a cup of tea and a pie, and pretend to fly a plane?"
*Pete Bemmer*

# Strange shops

**Above left:** "This New Zealand shop sells jumpers – the term 'one size fits all' is very apt."
*Champaklal Lad*

**Above right:** "I saw this weird model in a shop in Kunming, Yunnan, China. I didn't find out what the model means, as the shop assistant didn't speak English, but I thought it was a great, eye-catching way to advertise the trousers. My caption would be: "Dress for Success – Wear Victory Pants!" "
*Heather Shirra*

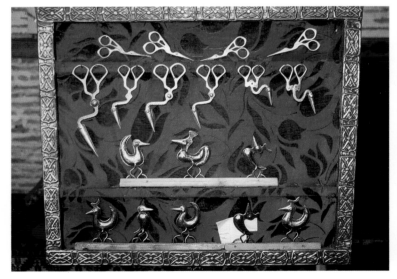

**Far left:** There's some strange snipping going on in Bukhara, Uzbekistan.
*Paul Morrison*

**Left:** "China has the most amazing signs. Some of the names of restaurants were downright strange – this was one of my favourites, in Xi'an: Sunny Half Past 8 Friend Changing Club."
*Sophie Atkinson*

**Top:** "These toys were in a shop in Antigua, Guatemala. During the Day of the Dead, you choose the model that best represents the character of your departed loved one to honour their spirit."
*Anne Siller*

**Above:** "The main market in Lima's bustling Barrio Chino is full of people buying meat, fruit, veg, fish – everything you could possibly want to eat. Yet there was this stall, too, entirely devoted to selling plastic food."
*Gregory Froome*

**Above right & right:** "I found this toy of Bush chasing Bin Laden for sale on the streets of Marrakesh, Morocco."
*Kiki Streitberger*

**Left & below left:** "Cows hang from the ceiling of this shop on Dam Square, Amsterdam."
*Rebecca Burright*

**Below, far left:** "Wearing a top made of condoms, this lady is on display in a Bangkok 'restaurant-cum-shop' that is involved in AIDS prevention campaigns and fundraising. An unusual way to send the message out!"
*Alessandra Ferraris*

**Right:** "On the road to the Bay of Fires, Tasmania, there are plenty of original letterboxes. This was accompanied by a message on a cardboard sign. One bag or two?"
*Carlota Godinho*

**Far right:** "Taken outside the ruins of Ephesus in Turkey... interesting use of the words 'genuine' and 'fake' to describe their watches!"
*Giulietta Valuri*

**Below right:** "Crackers appeared on the menus of most bus journeys in Argentina. I went into a supermarket in Salta and saw a whole aisle consisting solely of crackers!"
*Kirsty Wilson*

**Far right, below:** "Iguana poncho, Trieste, Italy." Well, you wouldn't want your iguana to get wet, would you?
*Samantha Dobson*

HORSE POO 50¢ Per Bag

GENUINE FAKE WATCHES

iguana Poncho
Includes 40" Lizard Leash

# }Freaky flavours

## TRUE STORIES:
### cat casserole

"**M**y first experience of Borneo's cuisine was at the Dynasty Hotel in Sarawak. My stay there would have been unmemorable were it not for the fish lips they offered as an appetiser. Fish lips?!

My culinary tour continued in Gunung Mulu National Park where, after days of nothing but steamed rice and vegetables, we were served casserole. The surgeon in our group carefully studied the chunks of meat and declared the mystery ingredient to be of feline origin.

Two days later the clunk of a machete signalled that the cook was preparing another casserole. By now I had started to think that our surgeon had been mistaken. The previous casserole had certainly consisted of something unusual – but cat? Where would you find a cat in the Bornean jungle?

Clunk, clunk, clunk... Despite the butchery in the background, the park was an overwhelmingly peaceful place. As I sat in quiet contemplation of my surroundings, deep within the rainforest, the shadow of Gunung Mulu looming over me, the tranquillity was broken by a loud 'miaaaaooow'!

A terrified cat shot out of the kitchen, between my legs and disappeared at breakneck speed into the jungle.

On our last night we ate in Kota Kinabalu's main square where, amongst the red snapper, lobster and crab proudly displayed in the restaurants' large glass tanks, sat a large plastic tub of toads: pondweed green, bulbous and warty. I took one look at this seething amphibian mass – and ordered steamed rice and vegetables. After three weeks in Borneo, fish lips didn't sound so strange after all."

*Professor Yaffle, on www.goWander.com*

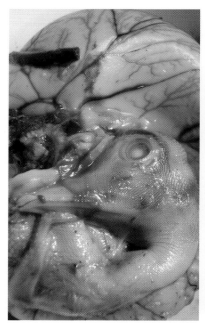

**Top left:** "I found these beers in Kanab, Utah, USA – Mormon country. The signs said: 'Why have just one!' and 'Bring some home for the wives!' and made me laugh so hard – it was nice that the producers had a sense of humour about this taboo subject. It was tasty beer, too!"
*Sophie Atkinson*

**Far left:** "On long-distance trains in Vietnam, one of the delicacies often hawked through the carriages is a duck egg boiled with a partially developed embryo inside."
*Gavin Fernandes*

**Left:** "Perusing the shelves of a local supermarket for a few travel snacks in the beautiful town of Shangri-La, China, I stumbled across this tasty morsel – vacuum-packed pig snout. Taste-tastic!"
*Flynn Lund*

**Above:** "Eyes glued to the Kalahari in north-eastern Namibia, following tracks indistinguishable to our eyes, the bushmen eventually came to a termite mound where the nocturnal porcupine was sleeping inside. After digging a hole three bodies long, they wormed in and chased out the animal, spearing him as he ran through tall grass. Dinner!"
*Kim Walker*

**Right:** "I was a little alarmed to see some perfectly preserved seahorses for sale at this market in Hanoi, Vietnam. They are sold in pairs – one male and one female, tied together with rubber bands – for medicinal purposes."
*Sophie Atkinson*

**Far left, top:** "The Bulgarian method of cooking red peppers."
*Emilie Kamanova*

**Left, top:** The thirsty in the Outback will always remember Karl...
*Andrew Swaffer*

**Far left, below:** "We had to smile when we saw the two colas next to each other, the Muslim version and the American version, in a small shop in Gilgit, northern Pakistan. The small print on the bottles – 'The taste of freedom' and 'Dare for more' seemed so ironic."
*Nadine Hudson*

**Left, below:** "His and hers optics at the Seeheim Hotel, Namibia. Drop in before tackling the long gravel drive to the Fish River Canyon. It's an old railhead hotel, full of character, with stuffed big-game heads on the walls – but it's the impala male-and-female optics that attract thirsty travellers!"
*Joseph Brennan*

**Above:** "These iguanas at a market in Granada, Nicaragua, are not for sale as pets but rather for dinner. In Belize they call iguana meat 'bamboo chicken'."
*Seth Andersen*

**Left:** "Those Germans aren't stereotyped as sausage eaters for nothing! This sausage seller in Frankfurt had a grill attached to his waist so he could prepare a meat treat wherever he went – not forgetting an attachable umbrella to complete the contraption, rendering it weatherproof!"
*Natalie Finlayson*

**Below far left:** "While visiting the local chemist for medical supplies in Quito, Ecuador, we spotted this interestingly branded product – though we have no idea if it lives up to its promise!"
*Claire Cockcroft*

**Below left centre:** "While trekking the Annapurna Circuit in Nepal, we stayed overnight in the village of Kagbeni. Exploring the dusty streets, one of our party was fantasising about a Big Mac after weeks of *dal bhat*. We turned a corner and... his prayer was answered. Big Yac, Nepalese style!"
*Phil Crouch-Baker*

**Below left:** "In Switzerland the Matterhorn is used everywhere for marketing purposes – even on bread."
*Markus Kaufmann*

# }Signs: food for thought

STRONG VIOLENT SPIRITS
洋酒

|  | | GL/杯 | BTL |
|---|---|---|---|
| | | | 40 |
| Chivas Regal 12 Years | 芝华士 | | — |
| Chivas Regal (small bottle) | 芝华士 (小瓶) | | |

**Bushmans menu**

TODAYS SPECIAL ... is yesterday's leftovers

BREAKFAST SERVED @ BREAKFAST TIME
• FULL BREAKFAST    $10·50
• PANCAKE  $3  • BAGELS $4·50
LUNCH SERVED @ LUNCHTIME
• BAMBI BURGERS $9·~
• SHOVEL FLIPPED ROADSIDE PIZZA  $4·50
• ROADKILL TOASTED SANDWICHES    $7·50
• BORING REGULAR TOASTED SANDWICHES  $5·~
• SOUP OF THE DAY.. $6~
DINNER  IF You're here at Dinnertime you'll be charged with Breaking & ENTERING.

MILKSHAKES $4~
FILTER COFFEE $2·80
RADIATOR TEA $2·80
BREAKFAST TEA $2·80
HERBAL TEAS  $2·80
HOT CHOCOLATE $3·50
HOT BLACKCURRANT $3~

WILD GAME PIES $4~
ROAD KILL POSSUM PIES $4~
FRUIT SALAD BOWL $5~
FRESH SCONES & MUFFINS EVERY MORNING

以下食品請到"自選閣"領取
Please Take From " Daily Selection "

| 5.50 | 豬紅 Pig Blood |
| 5.50 | 豬皮 Pig Skin |
| 5.50 | 鳳爪 Chicken Feet |

| 3122 | 沸騰水煮魚 .... Boiled Fish Filet in Sichuan 激辣水煮鱼 |
| 3123 | 辣子鸡中翅 Spicy Chicken Wings 唐辛子風味の鶏手羽 |
| 3124 | 香辣馋嘴牛蛙 .... Spicy Bull Frog スパイシーウシガエル |
| 3125 | 香辣拌木耳 .... Spicy Jew's Ear キクラゲのピリ辛和え |
| 3126 | 麻辣鸡丝凉粉 .... Spicy Rice Noodle with 太春雨入り辛ロバンバンジー |

Today
> Foods
> Snake
> Desserts
> Wine
> Cocktails

SAUSAGE
SALAMI
HAM
BACON
TENDER LION
PRIME  TAIL
BEKTI FISH
PRAWN
CHICKEN BREAST

PRASUMA

BIN LADEN
BUNS
BREAD

Isabel Hopkins; Lauren Laman; Maude Hallé Saint-Cyr; Myra Needleman; Mick Walton; Peter Ransay; Marilyn Wittwohl

# )Signs: shops

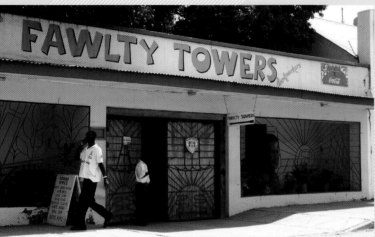

# Surreal
## wheels

So much more than getting from A to B: test-drive the planes, trains and buses that are just that little bit different

F 120

**Hot ticket:** "This mini fire engine was on an emergency call in Cheung Chau, Hong Kong – a normal vehicle would be unable to negotiate the winding alleys of the market."
*Chris Prior*

# Strange notions of motions

Transport is boring. Gone are the days when horse carts, triple-masted schooners and plushly mahoganied rail carriages were the height of conveyance chic; in the 21st century we spend most of our time using (barely) functional commuter trains, no-frills airlines and comfy-but-dull family saloons. Even Concorde, the lone dash of 70s aviation pizzazz, has been forced into retirement. We can get around easier than ever, but it's just not so much *fun*.

Or is it?

For every boring British bus, there's a rickety chicken-bus equivalent, piled high with a health-and-safety-horrifying number of men, women, their kids, their goats, their goats' kids and their shopping. Not to mention the fact that the bus has to negotiate potholed roads with three flat tyres and Bob Marley blasting from the (crackly) stereo.

And for every yellow US school bus there are almost as many variations as there are countries: you could be pedalled to your classes by a turban-topped rickshaw-wallah, or propelled through estuarine waters by an outboard motor. Yours could be pulled by a donkey, or a camel, or a two-stroke tractor engine. It could be rainbow-hued or covered with tassels.

The fact is that taking local transport is possibly the best way of getting a true glimpse of everyday life in another country – meeting the passengers, admiring the accoutrements and decorations inside, and watching the world go by as you go by the world.

People have always been proud (often obsessively so) of their vehicles – whether they're powered by an animal or a machine – and go to extraordinary lengths to make them stand out. Among all the regular car-owners there are plenty of crackpots who've painted their ride pink/covered it in grass/stretched it to six times its original length/stuck a water-spewing fountain on the bonnet – just for the hell of it.

And be it souped up, puttering out or downright odd, transport is what makes your travel possible – even if, often, the vehicle is so improbable.

**Cuban cuties:** "Buzzing and bouncing around Havana's roads in 'Cocos' is an experience – it's not just for the tourists: locals use them, too."
*Steve Morgan*

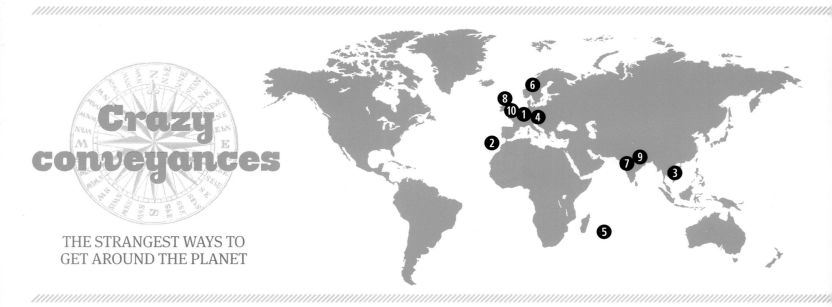

# Crazy conveyances

## THE STRANGEST WAYS TO GET AROUND THE PLANET

# TRANSPORT TRIVIA

➔ Police in Chongqing, China, feed drivers raw chillies to help them stay awake on the road

➔ Lloyd Scott cycled across Australia on a Penny Farthing – dressed as Sherlock Holmes

➔ The first flight from Europe to Asia was in the 17th century – Ahmet Celebi glided over the Bosphorus wearing fake wings

❶ **Pedal pub, Amsterdam** Taking drinking and 'driving' to a new level, this mobile hostelry is powered by up to 17 cyclists who can sup from the central bar as they bike.

❷ **Toboggan, Madeira** Ernest Hemingway deemed this one of his most exhilarating experiences – and who are we to argue? Whizz down from the town of Monte in an over-size basket on runners, just like Papa used to.

❸ **Bamboo train, Cambodia** These wooden platforms propelled by puttering generators reach up to 40km/h. But there's only one line, so if two happen to meet, the lightest is lifted off the rails to make way.

❹ **Children's Railway, Budapest** It looks like a regular train. It moves like a regular train. But all staff bar the engine driver on this Hungarian service are aged between ten and 14.

❺ **Underwater sub-scooter, Mauritius** Explore the seabed while breathing naturally – seated on a contraption straight out of a James Bond movie.

❻ **Bike lift, Trondheim, Norway** Too tired to pedal? Click your bicycle into the world's only lift dedicated to two-wheeled travellers, saving you 130m of uphill toil.

❼ **Pulley bridge, India** The only way over some of the raging rivers of the Himalaya is in a pendulous basket, pulled over the rapids by a rudimentary hand winch. Gulp.

❽ **Falkirk Wheel, Scotland** It takes an ingenious solution to link two canals that are 35 vertical metres apart – so enter the planet's only rotating boat lift, which scoops vessels out of one waterway and deposits them in the other.

❾ **Parahawking, Nepal** Take to the skies in a regular, engine-free paraglider with a trained bird of prey for company. As the hawk finds the thermals to help it soar, you can follow.

❿ **DUKW, London** Is it a bus? Or is it a boat? These amphibious trucks – like army landing vehicles for troops – deliver tourists directly from road to river.

# Pimp my ride

## TRUE STORIES:
### Pakistan's tarted-up trucks

"**A**s we pulled into the lay-by, I don't know who was more curious – us four female travellers or the conflab of gossiping truckers that we'd stopped to talk to.

I don't normally frequent truck stops but along Pakistan's iconic Karakoram Highway the vehicles are something else. Though their engines may be spluttering, they look a million dollars.

"Who will hire me to transport their load if my truck looks no good?" one of the men explained to us with a shrug. Consequently, spectacular is the order of the day: each panel is painted with lurid countryside scenes and curly Koranic verse; well-polished hubcaps sparkle with punched-metal flowers; pom-poms dangle from every rim and mirror; and bumpers jangle with fringes of bells.

"Want to see inside?" the driver next to me asked.

Up in the cab there were more automotive bows and whistles. Multi-coloured lights flashed around the dash and windscreen like a 1970s mobile disco while just above the steering wheel were three big buttons – the driver motioned for me to go ahead, press: three different horn tones! All very, *very* loud.

With all the fluorescence, twirling and comedy noises, the overall effect was as if a child had been asked to come up with their perfect car and got out the full pack of felt tips.

I was just about to jump down from the tattered driver's seat when something moved behind my shoulder – it was a live kestrel. Of course it was – what self-respecting driver transporting precious cargo between China and the Punjab doesn't need a pet bird for company?

After 20 minutes or so we left the truckers to their gossiping and climbed back into our comfy, modern, white (birdless) minivan – with only one horn. Now, where's the fun in that?"
*Sarah Baxter*

**"Something moved behind my shoulder – it was a kestrel. Of course it was – what self-respecting driver doesn't need a pet bird for company?"**

**Temples to transport:** "In Pakistan, drivers spend small fortunes blinging up their trucks – their steeds are the only things they lavish more attention on than their moustaches."
*Sarah Baxter*

**Top left:** "I found this car sitting on Robson Street in Vancouver, British Columbia. It is packed with pieces of art and writing connected to Canada. One of the highlights is definitely the little fountain running in the centre of the bonnet."
*Esther Gellings*

**Far left, below:** "Decorating your chicken bus is very, very important to all of the bus drivers in Central America. I spotted this one in San Marcos, Guatemala. Wonder where he found those Texas licence plates?"
*Seth Andersen*

**Below left:** "Cambodians go out in style with fantastic colourful hearses, quite unlike the boring black ones of the Western world."
*Rhoda Allen*

**Right:** "I found this 'green' car in east London. To see a car covered with grass – even an eco-friendly model like this Smart car – took me by surprise!"
*Graham Berridge*

**Far right, top:** "I spotted this souped-up Lada in Havana – it's a common sight throughout Cuba and much of Central America. No car is safe from a spoiler and decal attack!"
*Lucy Jefferys*

**Far right, below:** "The Dutch are famous for their artwork. I found this revealing example on the side of a barge, which had obviously seen better days, in Amsterdam."
*Lesley Heptinstall*

# }Going nowhere fast

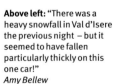

**Above left:** "There was a heavy snowfall in Val d'Isere the previous night – but it seemed to have fallen particularly thickly on this one car!"
*Amy Bellew*

**Above right:** "I took this amazing pic in Mérida, Yucatán, Mexico, in the city's modern art museum."
*Francois Ouellet*

**Right:** "On a fantastic trip around the salt flats and altiplano of southern Bolivia, one of the highlights was a trip to a train graveyard just a few miles outside Uyuni. Dozens of carriages lie rusting at the edge of the large salt flat; some are perfectly preserved."
*Sophie Atkinson*

**Opposite, top right:** "This is obviously a staged 'work of art'. However, not everybody was to know this when I emailed the photo home and made up an elaborate story about a bizarre accident with my hire car."
*Eugene McLaughlin*

**Opposite, below left:** "Someone was really angry with the owner of this car! OK, it was actually part of a city-wide installation of pieces for Reykjavík Art Week in Iceland."
*Hayley Dunning*

**Opposite, below right:** The Australian Outback is home to some intriguing wrecks.
*Andrew Swaffer*

**Above:** "Nobody was paying any attention to the bulldozer in Havana, Cuba – they just kept on working... or talking."
*Judy Palmaers*

**Above right:** "How did it get there? That's what I wondered when I spotted this car in Varanasi, India."
*Kiki Streitberger*

**Right:** "What does this bridge do? What two points should it be connecting? At the moment this photo was taken it was adrift on the Amsterdam-Rhine Canal by Utrecht, the Netherlands."
*Tim Brierley*

# }Filling up

**Above left:** "Petrol takeaway – along Cambodian roads you can find these colourful gas stations. Petrol is also sold in 1L bottles, depending on your needs. Safety is definitely not an issue here!"
*Alessandra Ferraris*

**Left:** "I came across this petrol station at Marloth Park, Mpumalanga, South Africa – everything except a tiger in the tank! Before we started our safari, we filled up the car from unleaded elephant; meanwhile, the diesel leopard kept a watchfuel eye. It's not every garage that can blend into its environment so successfully!"
*Anne Siller*

**Top right:** "The only gas station for *many* miles leaving Chile and entering Argentina on our way to El Chaltén."
*Jim Pratt*

**Above:** "Filling station in Saga, western Tibet. The pumps are inside the booth, with hoses passed through the windows!"
*Peter Ramsay*

# }Busman's holiday

## TRUE STORIES: India by bus

**B**eing British, I have a rather well-defined (read: reserved) sense of my own personal space. I'm pretty keen on privacy, and feel certain things – belching, hocking phlegm and farting, for instance – are not appropriate in the public domain. Which may explain why I was finding this Indian bus journey so, er, challenging.

Initially it was the sliding window – that wouldn't stay shut – which vexed me the most. (Never mind the fact that my knees were up where my nose should be, my nose itself being diverted out of the unclosable window to seek solace from the great unwashed within...). But soon it was the cacophony of trumps, snorts and eructations that had my British back up. As dusk turned into darkness, the bus's organic orchestra ratcheted up a notch: nasal clearing of deafening volume and unabashed flatulence filled the air.

And then began the choir of snoring: falsetto, soprano, baritone... all were represented, gradually falling into time as if arranged by some invisible conductor. I looked around at my cramped companions in disbelief. How was anyone getting any sleep in here?

It got worse. As the bus rattled on its nighttime journey, we would make occasional stops at the Indian equivalent of motorway service stations. Only they were less Little Chef, more large rave.

Regardless of the hour (1am, 3am, 4am...), the crackly, high-pitched radio would be turned up to 11, blaring bhangra to a mass of people – what were they all doing here at this ungodly hour? What? WHAT?!

Cigarettes were smoked, horns blared, topics argued, unidentifiable foods fried, all in our brief pockets of unmoving moments in those darkest witching hours.

When the sun *finally* started to rise and I came round from my half-sleep, I wasn't even sure we'd stopped at all, I'd been travelling so long. Then the man in front of me let out a mighty, reverberating burp. Ah, yes: back to reality..."

*Holly Beresford*

## "The bus's orchestra ratcheted up a notch: nasal clearing of deafening volume & unabashed flatulence"

Propelled By Clean Fuel

**Opposite, right:** " 'Clean fuel'?? This is a 'clean' bus on the streets of Delhi!"
*Andrei Gorodilov*

**Opposite far left & above:** "One careful owner? I took these shots in Laos – and there were plenty of other contenders!"
*Mick Walton*

**Above left:** "A destination board that could be mistaken for a safety instruction on this bus in Hong Kong."
*Chris Prior*

**Left:** "This picture taken in Agra, India, shows an old man driving a rickshaw. What is impressive about this photo is the 11 well-dressed students that he's carrying – instead of two, as recommended!"
*Nicolas Lepoutre*

**Opposite:** "I spotted this school 'bus' in Varanasi, India, after having enjoyed the sunrise over the Ganges. All sorts of bikes and trikes were going past, but this chap was hauling at least 12 kids to the WHSmith Memorial School."
*Anthony Robson*

**Above left:** "I just loved this three-wheeled... thing... steered by a tiller! I saw it in Takab, north-west Iran."
*Chris Beggs*

**Below left:** "Taken in the suburbs of Lahore, Pakistan. There are no public transport companies here as in Europe, but each bus is owned privately. The decoration of buses (as well as trucks) is a real art. Paintings represent landscapes, religious scenes, local beliefs... the shapes and colours are fascinating – as well as the number of people travelling on it!"
*Nicolas Lepoutre*

**Below:** "How to get a canoe on a bus... Canoeing is a popular pastime in Norfolk. It was obvious that the green-minded rowers would like to go by bus – however, have you ever tried to get a canoe on a bus?!"
*Ian Dinmore*

# }Fully loaded

**Far left, top:** "I was in a taxi outside Battambang, Cambodia, and saw this guy coming. He was moving pretty fast, even though he looks like he is about to tip over."
*Sean MacLeod*

**Left:** "School boat on Seribu Island, Jakarta, Indonesia."
*Willy Souw*

**Far left, below:** "Vietnamese Orange Tree Transportation Ltd! One of many Hanoi residents taking an orange tree home, precariously balanced on the back of his rickety moped, for Tet (New Year) celebrations."
*Stuart Young*

**Left centre:** I loved the way this guy outside the velodrome in Baku, Azerbaijan, made sure he was not going to run out of apples to sell from his car. I guess he was expecting a rush."
*Chris Mills*

**Below left:** "Overloaded with baskets in George, South Africa."
*Mel Wreford*

**Right:** "The people in Vietnam pack everything possible on their motorbikes – refrigerators, sofas, balls and heavy flowerpots, like these in Hanoi."
*Julia Lövenich*

**Below:** "I was in a tuk tuk in Siem Reap, Cambodia, when I was confronted by these pigs on the back of a scooter – not an everyday occurrence where I come from…"
*Joanne Hare*

# Animal magic

**Top left:** "The idea of these 'ships of the desert' strapped down and transported in the back of a pick-up truck, three abreast, near Aswan in Egypt, was very strange!"
*Gregory Froome*

**Top right:** "Taking a ride on a camel is a common option – but here the camels were the ones enjoying the ride."
*Anne Frigon*

**Above left:** "This picture is the result of a publicity stunt at Great Yarmouth station in Norfolk, UK, to promote Christmas shopping by train."
*Ian Dinmore*

**Above right:** "In the small Egyptian oasis town of Siwa, this enterprising young man was offering transportation the local way."
*Anne Frigon*

**Opposite, main image:** "Assamese traffic, India."
*Adam Vaught*

**Opposite, below left:** "Goldfish on wheels, Beijing."
*Danielle Rippingale*

**Opposite, below centre:** Very fresh fish: "This 'mobile fridge' pulled up by the road at Gurah, Sumatra, Indonesia."
*Martine Ashmore*

**Opposite, below right:** "There are many such 'bikes of burden' in Vietnam, carrying a variety of goods, from ducks to baskets – to live fish."
*Marie Timmermans*

# }Just odd

**Above left:** "On the Ganges at Varanasi, India, I came across this floating TV – the pay-per-view system applied 'Indian' style."
*Ewa Sierzynska*

**Left:** "Coming out of Gower Gulch in Death Valley, California, we arrived at Badwater (the lowest place in North America) to see this rider, somehow looking odd – but also totally fitting in this strange, grand landscape."
*Janet Morgan*

**Top:** "2 BE and NOT 2B – serendipity or statement?"
*Graham Berridge*

**Above:** "The Uros people of Lake Titicaca make realistic Cat-amarans around Puno, Peru."
*Ben Moulam*

**Right:** "We finally came to the end of a four-day drive through Mongolia from Ulaanbaatar to Khövsgöl to find 2,760 sq km of frozen lake. We passed this ship, *Sukhbaatar*, encapsulated in the ice as we drove the 36km across the ice to the other side."
*Ryan Snell*

# }Road signs & signals

# Eccentric
## animals

If all the world's a stage, wildlife usually
hogs the limelight – this technicolour show
has a cast of billions of bizarre beasts

**Pup in boots:** "This dog was having a brief respite when I found him in Chelsea, New York City. The look on his face made it extremely evident that he did not like being made to wear shoes."
*Jesper Mattias*

# If only they could talk...

It's said that legends of the cyclops stemmed from discoveries of mammoths' skulls, and that narwhal tusks prompted tales of single-horned unicorns. Scientists' recreations of dinosaurs depict creatures with scaly wings, huge crests, spines and plates, spiked club tails and long, snaking necks.

But whatever bizarre beasts roamed the earth millions of years ago – or, more recently, in our imaginations – there are plenty of biological marvels being discovered even today that make the eyes widen (and, sometimes, the stomach churn).

Over the centuries, hoaxes have been created with the intention of fooling naive scientists – yet who'd conceive of such a bizarre beast as the platypus? Not those academics who on first seeing a specimen declared it a botched faux-animal, sewn together from parts of other creatures. So who's to say the yeti doesn't exist? Visit the hairy hominid's 'scalp' in Nepal and you could yet be convinced.

Then there are giants – monstrous tortoises in the Seychelles and Galápagos Islands, flowers a metre and more across, stag beetles as large as dinner plates, giant anteaters and otters scurrying across the savannahs and wetlands of South America – and miniatures: frogs the size of fingernails, minuscule marmosets and even pygmy hippos.

And of course, it's not all about appearances. Plants and animals behave in ways that amuse and bewilder, from the snapping jaws of carnivorous venus flytraps to the near-human antics of apes, monkeys and dolphins. Sloths so slow algae grow in their fur discover, too late, their destination is not actually a tree. Penguins audition to be film stars at the South Pole.

The natural world constantly confounds our expectations and perceptions, and with more and more people travelling to exotic climes with cameras, we're all becoming wildlife photographers. Keep an eye out for that cyclops – the next front cover could be yours...

**By a nose:** The nasal splendour of the male proboscis monkey – his nose can grow to 18cm – is designed to attract the ladies. For these guys in the forests of Borneo, size matters.
*Sandra Dean*

# Weird wildlife worldwide

WHAT TO SPOT WHERE ON
YOUR GLOBAL WANDERINGS

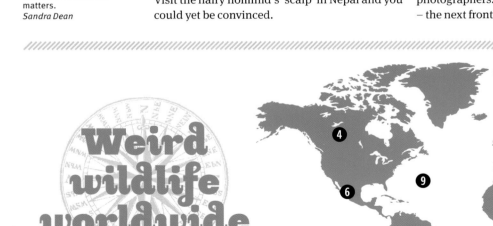

**❶ Blob fish, Tasmania, Australia** Critters don't come much grumpier or uglier than this deep-sea resident, mostly made up of jelly-like material to survive the extreme pressures of its 1,000m-below habitat.

**❷ Narwhal, Arctic** Also known as the Arctic unicorn, this rarely seen white whale has a long, twisted tooth-horn that extends up to 2m from the front of its mouth.

**❸ Sloth, Latin America** Redefines sloooow... with its diet of mostly indigestible leaves, a full sloth stomach can make up two-thirds of its weight. The sloth is so slow-moving that algae grow on its fur.

**❹ Star-nosed mole, Canada & USA** With 22 pink tentacles bursting from its little schnoz, this mole can feel for its prey, tunnel, swim and generally get on with life – all without sight.

**❺ Aye-aye, Madagascar** Winner in the Gollum look-alike stakes, this nocturnal primate finds its food by tapping on trees, gnawing a hole then scooping out grubs and insects with its bony middle finger.

**❻ Axolotl, Mexico** This salamander with feathery pink gills doesn't just look odd – it can regrow not only limbs, but also parts of its brain.

**❼ Okapi, Democratic Republic of Congo** With reddish back and black-and-white horizontal stripes on its legs, this half-zebra, half-giraffe has another trick – it can wash its own eyes and ears with its tongue.

**❽ Proboscis monkey, Borneo** With a bulging belly comprising about a quarter of its whole body weight, the male proboscis sports a pendulous nose, up to 18cm long, which reportedly attracts females.

**❾ Hag fish, worldwide** Known as the 'slime eel', the hag fish isn't actually an eel – but it *is* slimy, secreting vast quantities of mucus in order to escape tight spots. Oh, and it has four hearts and two brains...

**❿ Platypus, Australia** This bizarre mishmash – duck's bill, beaver's tail, otter's feet, poisonous spur – was originally believed to be an elaborate hoax, sewn together from the body parts of various animals.

# }Beastly behaviour

## Monkey business

In 2008 a storm broke in the Tinseltown teacup when the world's longest-living non-human primate – a 76-year-old chimp – published his autobiography. Yes, you read right: Cheeta, co-star of the Tarzan films of the 1930s and 1940s, caused a furore by taking potshots at Hollywood grandees including Rex Harrison, Charlie Chaplin and Mickey Rooney in his memoirs.

Memoirs? A chimpanzee? Well... *Me Cheeta* was, of course, ghostwritten. But though this book was a good-natured literary hoax, human fascination with the behaviour of our closest relatives – apes and monkeys – has led to some pretty unusual results.

Attempts to teach primates to communicate using forms of language have long been reported. In the mid-1960s a chimp named Washoe was taught a range of 'words' using American Sign Language; other subjects followed, including a lowland gorilla called Koko, the bonobo (pygmy chimpanzee) Kanzi, an orang-utan called Chantek and several other chimps, including the wittily named Nim Chimpsky.

With dextrous hands and expressive faces, it's easy to believe primates communicate in similar ways to us. But primate behaviour is fascinating (and often odd) enough in itself. For example, squirrel monkeys smear food on their tails with their hands, probably to aid identification of family members; the calls of howler monkeys can be heard over a distance of 5km; and, like adolescent humans, male gorillas like to show off at the pool, launching themselves into the water with gigantic splashes to signal their strength. Boys, boys, boys...

> ## "Like adolescent humans, male gorillas like to show off at the pool, launching themselves into the water"

**Opposite:** Just catching up on my current affairs... The monkeys around Victoria Falls, Zambia, are a highbrow bunch.
*Barry O'Sullivan*

**Above left:** Ah, Coke break! "I was in a camp in the jungle of Sabah, Borneo, and this cheeky little devil grabbed a Coke can inadvertently left in front of one of our huts. It then jumped on the clothes line to drink it without being disturbed."
*Alessandra Ferraris*

**Above right:** When the monkeys in Gibraltar aren't lounging around, picking each others' toenails, they're likely to be jumping on your car bonnet, posing for photos.
*Weronika Nowicka*

**Below far left:** 'Will you two please shut up and let me sleep?!' Life's tough for Gibraltar's macaque mums.
*Weronika Nowicka*

**Below left:** Ouch! Breast-feeding doesn't look much fun for Burma's monkey mothers.
*Kyaw Thar*

This page: "Mr, Mrs and Junior Marine Iguana pose for a beautiful family shot in the Galápagos… only faintly less weird than the courtship 'dance' of huge albatross (*above*) and the antics of blue-footed boobies."
*Pete Browning*

Opposite, top & below right: "The emperor penguins of Snow Hill, Antarctica, loved our camera equipment." *Laurie Allread*

Opposite, below middle: "My friend was blissfully unaware of her Adélie penguin spectators in Antarctica, which had waddled over." *Dr Jonathan Grey*

Opposite, below far left: "I tripped over the hefty chops of this tonne of adolescent elephant seal outside my hut at Davis Station, Antarctica, one night. He farted and belched for 48 hours, flummoxed by the 15cm-high barrier. His 'body music' rendered sleep nigh on impossible." *Dr Jonathan Grey*

# Nature gone nuts

We all love penguins. The waddle. The dinner suits. The vast colonies. But not many people know that penguins aren't solely resident in Antarctic climes; there's one species that paddles on the equator – the Galápagos penguin, on its eponymous islands.

Stranded 1,000km west of mainland Ecuador, the Galápagos Islands are pretty, well, unusual. For starters, there are no native land mammals, just lizards and giant tortoises. The theory? A few tortoises and lizards somehow fell into the ocean and floated on flotsam and jetsam to the only land around for thousands of miles.

This scenario, coupled with favourable currents and millennia of isolation, has created an archipelago with a magical, if unusual, selection of wildlife. Take the marine iguana. Found

nowhere else on earth, these black, scaly mini-dragons bask in hundred-strong piles, soaking up rays and projectile-snorting seawater out of their nostrils – something they have to do, due to being the world's only amphibious lizard – after grazing the seabed for algae.

Then there are the birds: all wonderfully weird. From the bulbous red pouch of the male frigatebird (his way of saying, "Hello, ladies"), to the ridiculously blue-footed booby to the elaborately choreographed mating dance of the waved albatross, the avian residents are a colourful and quirky crew.

Best of all? The menagerie's lack of fear. The wildlife of the Galápagos doesn't run, swim or fly away; years of isolation mean it hasn't learned to fear man – perhaps the weirdest thing of all.

**Top left:** "A hyena chasing a seal at Namibia's Cape Cross seal colony. Or is it vice versa?"
*Renato Losio*

**Below, far left:** "There are a remarkable number of free-range chickens all over the Cayman Islands, even in downtown George Town. This one seemed to have definite ideas on how it wanted to be served up."
*Kirsi Peck*

**Below left:** "During a canal boat trip into the tropical jungles of Tortuguero National Park, Costa Rica, I spotted this emerald basilisk lizard just hanging out."
*Cyril Brass*

**Right:** "While exploring Kinabalu National Park, Borneo, our guide asked us if we'd like to see some *Rafflesia*. We paid a few ringgits to see these magnificent plants."
*Graham Racher*

**Centre right:** "Tab de way – a spongy red mushroom in Cancun, Mexico. It's known as 'Excrement of Xtabay' by the locals and as 'Witch's Vomit' in Spain. Its unpleasant smell is attractive to flies, which distribute its spores."
*Luisa Uruena*

**Far right:** "There's nothing like a nice, relaxing walk in the park... and this is *nothing* like a nice, relaxing walk in the park!" – strolling around the life-threatening Botanical Gardens in Athens, Greece.
*Jules Birkby*

# 10 OF THE WORLD'S STRANGEST PLANTS

**❶ *Rafflesia*, South-East Asia** The plant with the world's largest bloom (1m across) has a reddish-brown, fleshy flower and stinks like a rotting corpse.

**❷ *Azara microphylla*, Chile & Argentina** Not suitable for those on a diet, this small temptress of a tree smells like vanilla or white chocolate.

**❸ *Hydnora africana*, Africa** This vicious flower attacks the roots of nearby shrubs; it attracts carrion beetles with its putrid stench to aid pollination.

**❹ *Welwitschia mirabilis*, southern Africa** This plant never sheds its two leaves – they become tattered with age – up to 1,500 years.

**❺ Venus flytrap, USA** This carnivorous plant can trap its insect meal in 0.1 second before sealing its 'jaws' to digest its prey.

**❻ *Dracunculus vulgaris*, Europe** This friendly flower (the 'stink lily') releases a smell of rotting flesh to attract and trap flies.

**❼ *Wolffia angusta*, Australia** The world's smallest flowering plant; several could fit inside this 'o'.

**❽ *Wollemia nobilis*, Australia** Until 1994 this ancient tree was known only from 120-million-year-old fossils – there are fewer than 100 in the wild.

**❾ *Amorphophallus*, Pacific Islands** This plant's scientific title translates literally as 'shapeless male genitalia'. The clue's in the name...

**❿ *Nuytsia floribunda*, Australia** This parasitic tree attacks the roots of other plants – and sometimes, by mistake, underground cables.

# Odd animals

## Legendary creatures

Real creatures are all well and good – but what about the beasts that haven't made it into official encyclopaedias, despite being alive in the world's nightmares?

Yeti, Sasquatch, Yowie – tall tales of big, hairy ape-men roaming wilderness areas have been spun around campfires, chortens and billabongs for centuries. Despite numerous 'eyewitness' accounts, mysterious footprints in the snow, the appearance of grainy photos and even blurry film clips, no hard evidence has been found for the existence of these creatures. But that doesn't stop the legends circulating – and countless other beasts joining the pantheon.

The Jersey Devil is a bizarre two-legged winged creature that swoops through the air above New Jersey, USA – it's such a popular local legend that it's lent its name to a hockey team. Further south in the States, the Mothman made his/its appearances in the late 1960s around Charleston and Point Pleasant, West Virginia. A man-sized being with moth-like wings, flashing red eyes set into his chest and no head, the Mothman fluttered in then out of the limelight.

As well as being the name of the Australian yeti-like ape-man, Yowie is the tag for an Aboriginal beast – an ant-lizard cross with huge fangs and an appetite for midnight snacks, including people.

The Chinese have their own selection of hairy man-beasts: the Yeren or 'Man-Monkey', also known as the 'Wildman of Shennongjia', and the Ren Xiong – 'Man Bear' – a furball hiding in Hubei's high-level forests.

The most amusingly named creature, the Pukwudgie, lurks in the legends of the Wanpanoag people of North America. The Pukwudgie looks pretty much like a human – except for its big nose and ears, grey, glowing skin, and the fact that it's only a metre tall...

**"This man-sized being has moth-like wings, flashing red eyes set into his chest – and no head"**

THIS LAKE IS SACRED. DO NOT URINATE IN THE VICINITY OF THE LAKE.

**Above left:** "This is the famous 'yeti scalp' preserved and venerated in a Nepalese Monastery in Khumjung. It's a marvellous talking point."
*Andrew Heppleston*

**Below left:** A bad hair day for the birds of Budapest Zoo. At least, we think it's a bird...
*Amir Shimoni*

**Above:** Holy watering is forbidden at Tsongmo Lake, Sikkim, India. Let's hope someone told the yaks...
*Paul Belanger*

**Right:** "In Namibia's Etosha National Park we found the zebra that had lost its stripes!"
*Diane Blakeley*

**Far left, top:** Don't fancy yours much… "This camel at Woburn Safari Park, England, decided to give us a full display of his truly dreadful teeth."
*Eugene McLaughlin*

**Far left, centre:** "The big nose and large stomach of male proboscis monkeys is attractive to females… allegedly!"
*Sandra Dean*

**Far left, below:** "We saw Siamese turtles hatching on the beach of Perhentian Kecil, Malaysia."
*Robby Asnong*

**Middle left:** "Even locals get lost in the Australian Outback! This emu ponders a sign, wondering where to find its friends."
*Helen Whiting*

**Top left:** "Following our marriage, my husband and I conducted a Sri Satyanarayana *puja* (a two-hour Hindu ritual marking a new phase of life) in our shrine at home in Hyderabad, India. Little did we realise that the rabbit was using the remains to recreate his natural habitat!"
*Kate Bevan*

**Middle left:** "This British red letterbox in East Sussex, boarded up to stop anything being posted, created a perfect home for a family of snails. Mother snail, with baby snail, is on guard outside, while the rest of the family is snugly 'indoors'. Gives a new meaning to 'snail mail'!"
*Margit Latter*

**Below left:** "Vienna Zoo, Austria – home to the longest donkey I have ever seen!"
*Natalie Finlayson*

**Right:** "This poor three-toed sloth in Costa Rica had found himself in the most unlikely spot, confusing a traffic sign for a tree."
*Cyril Brass*

**Far left, top:** These Australian lizards are called thorny devils. Or should that be horny devils…?
*Andrew Swaffer*

**Far left, below:** "Cow grazing amid the tower blocks of Ulaanbaatar, Mongolia."
*Kris Weber*

**Above left, middle:** A trip to the optician may be due?
*Kyaw Thar*

**Top left:** "While searching for just the right place for a nude photo in the forests outside Santa Cruz, California, we came across this delightful banana slug, looking like he'd stepped out of *Alice in Wonderland*. He invited us for lunch."
*Janet Morgan*

**Middle left:** "This ring-tailed lemur was warming up in the sun without a trace of modesty! This was the sight facing us as we sat at breakfast on the veranda in Berenty Reserve, Madagascar."
*Sue Hirst*

**Centre left, below:** "When we woke up after a night of drinking somewhere in Thailand, we found this drunken frog struggling to get out of the glass."
*Robby Asnong*

**Below left:** 'I now pronounce you hound and wife' – canine coupling in Pennsylvania.
*Juraj Kaman*

**Above:** "Punta Tombo, near Trelew in Argentine Patagonia, is home to half a million Magellanic penguins. This cluster of penguins was so like humans – gathering round the no-smoking sign for a 'virtual' fag break!"
*Kris Weber*

**Top far left:** Ladybird love!
*Abe Heckenbach*

**Middle far left:** "Aliens have landed! I was taking a photograph of a lizard in Kruger, South Africa, when this grasshopper flew up onto the window of our lodge. Its face could have launched a thousand horror movies, but never got the chance... the lizard ate it."
*Anne Siller*

**Below far left:** Cirque du Scorpion? Arachnid acrobatics?
*Paul Morrison*

**Top left:** "There were thousands of ladybirds among the grassy sand dunes behind the beach – they seemed to be trying to seek shade from the midday sun."
*James Hill*

**Below left:** The world's most vivid caterpillar? Puerta Verde, Cancun, Mexico.
*Luisa Uruena*

**Top:** Mind the gap! "This intrepid praying mantis joined us round the pool in Kalkan, Turkey."
*Gizelle Gill*

**Right:** "I came across this long column of caterpillars in a park in Split, Croatia. It extended up and down a tree and then across the path – I never found the end. Unfortunately I stepped on the middle of it, separating it into two trails. I spent a while with a twig trying to join the trails back together, but had no success."
*Tom Charnock*

# }Signs: you know the rules

NO BOATS INCLUDING RUBBER DUCKS MAY PROCEED TO SEA WITHOUT A LAUNCH PERMIT

GEEN BOTE OF 'RUBBER DUCKS' MAG SEE TOE GAAN SONDER DIE NODIGE PERMIT

Уважаемые посетители музея-заповедника "Петропавловская крепость"! На территории музея запрещается:

Dear visitors to our museum Please be kindly advised that on the territory of the St.Peter and Paul Fortress you are not allowed to:

Просьба придерживаться правил и добро пожаловать в наш музей!

Please, strictly to our rules and welcome to our museum

A health worker has feelings too

Speak kindly to your doctor

NO TRESPASSING
Violators will be shot. Survivors will be shot again.

OUTSIDE EATABLES WILL BE PROSECUTED

严禁用自带食物喂鱼
PLEASE DO NOT FEED THE FISHES WITH YOUR PRIVATE

PLEASE
don't feed the Seagulls
or we will feed your children a DOUBLE ESPRESSO
Thanks

Bar Rules
酒吧条例
1 No drugs and fights inside
禁止吸毒及打架斗殴
2 Don't shit in our toilet but U can pee
本店卫生间只作'大便'
3 No wasting your drink at the bar
严禁浪费酒水，如有剩酒请喝干或倒
4 No Da Zhe but you can have a free drink on the house
没有折扣，本店已免送上此饮品供客人享用，请各位不要强求打折
5 No outside food or drinks allowed
禁止携带本店食品和饮料入场

Business Hour

929
COWBOY PARKING ONLY
VIOLATORS WILL BE CASTRATED

REMOVE NOTHING FROM THE ELEPHANTA ISLAND EXCEPT: NOURISHMENT FOR THE SOUL, CONSOLATION FOR THE HEART, INSPIRATION FOR THE MIND.
(FOREST DIVISION ALIBAG)

TOBACCO FREE ZOO
ধূমপান মুক্ত এলাকা
"প্রত্যাশা" মাদক বিরোধী সংগঠন

Please do not drop your cigarette butts on the deck.
The fish crawl out at night to smoke them and we are trying to get them to quit.

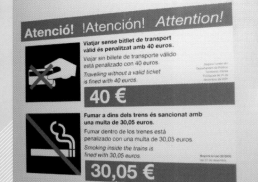
勿因一时疏忽
破坏永恒美好
A SINGLE ACT OF CARELESSNESS LEADS
TO THE ETERNAL LOSS OF BEAUTY

Atenció! ¡Atención! Attention!
Viatjar sense bitllet de transport vàlid és penalitzat amb 40 euros.
Viajar sin billete de transporte válido está penalizado con 40 euros.
Travelling without a valid ticket is fined with 40 euros.
40 €
Fumar a dins dels trens és sancionat amb una multa de 30,05 euros.
Fumar dentro de los trenes está penalizado con una multa de 30,05 euros.
Smoking inside the trains is fined with 30,05 euros.
30,05 €

If you are being chased by a BEAR...
DO NOT COME THROUGH THIS DOOR

DO NOT FLUCK FLOWERS
மலர்களை பறிக்காதீர்

When you tease, harass, touch, disturb or throw stones at them, they get angry and hurt just as you would.
Please treat animals with respect.

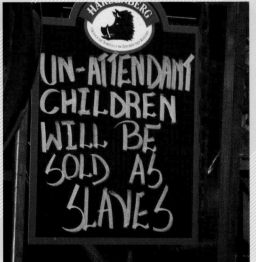
UN-ATTENDANT CHILDREN WILL BE SOLD AS SLAVES

# Crazed creations

Some art and architecture is intended to shock –
while some just raises an eyebrow (or a smile)

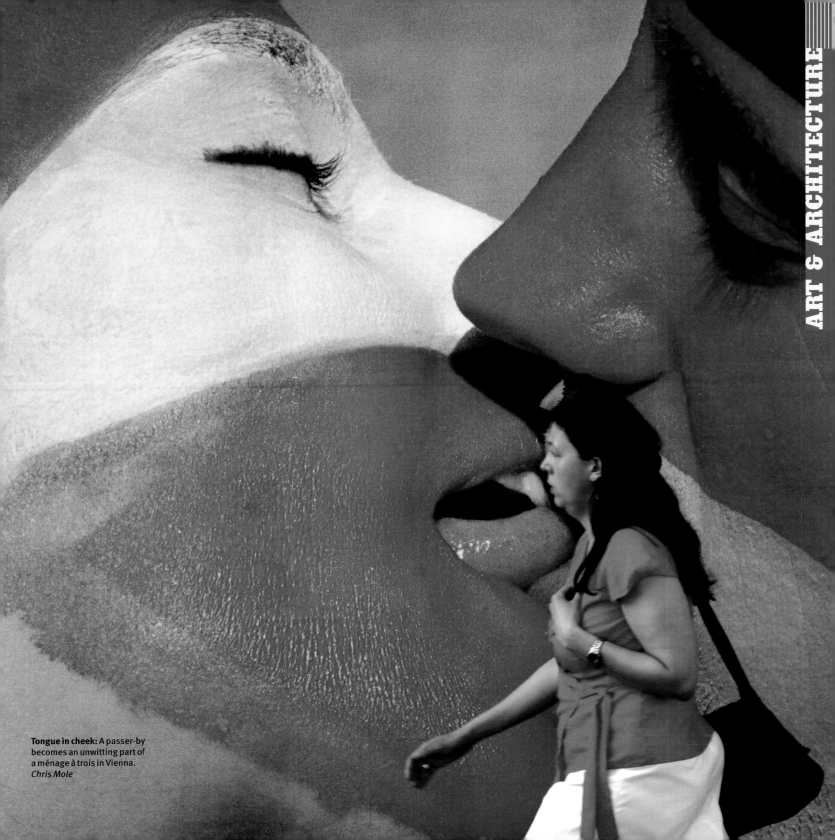

**Tongue in cheek:** A passer-by becomes an unwitting part of a ménage à trois in Vienna.
*Chris Mole*

# 'Art is a flock of sheep'

**W**inston Churchill said that, and when Winnie spoke, people listened. Of course, he wasn't literally suggesting that a bunch of baa-ing, wool-clad herbivores should be feted as an 'installation' in some leftfield gallery – he was actually discussing the roles of tradition and innovation in art.

But, as Damien Hirst (for one) has shown, there are plenty of quirky creative types around the planet looking at art – and sheep, for that matter – in a frankly skewed way. Whether the results are a cause for shock or celebration depends very much on your point of view.

Some see art in the everyday – and if it's not there already, they'll add it themselves. Graffiti artists have taken street art to new levels of novelty (or, in some cases, insanity) – in these pages, look for safety posts transformed into mock homicide scenes, giant ants invading public squares and disco cows shimmying through the streets.

Actually, there's something about cows that clearly inspires artists at the loopier end of the spectrum – and you don't need to slice them in half and pickle them in formaldehyde to make them eyecatching. Cows are built into walls; they're placed upside-down on shop ceilings; they're seen parading through cities the world over in many and astonishingly varied colours, shapes and patterns.

Other artists have decided that reality needs a bit of pepping up – Dalí led the way with his unique creations, but plenty of others have launched their own visions of surreality on the world: we've found derelict squats that have been transformed into dazzling installations; giant prawns, sheep and rocking horses and a range of other supremely unlikely objects looming over Antipodean landscapes; and deserts dotted with enormous Lego-like Barbie statues.

Why? Well, why not? We say: if it's different, and stands out from the norm, it's art. We're not sheep, after all.

**Relax in the arms of Jesus:** "It's nice to be able to sit down while shopping... This chair was for sale in a craft shop in Antigua, Guatemala; cocooned in the Lord's arms, the other pirate and businessman chairs became less alarming."
*Anne Siller*

# The world's weirdest buildings

ON THE QUEST OF
ARCHITECTURE GONE MAD

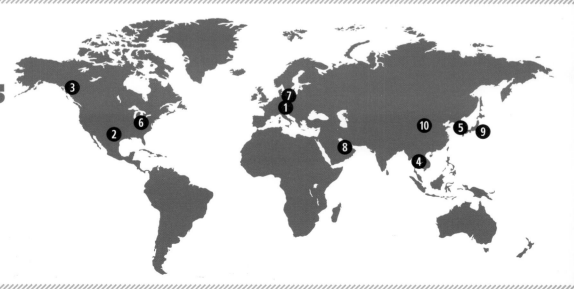

## BODGED BUILDINGS

➲ The vast Winchester Mystery House in California was under construction for 38 years... and never completed

➲ Officials spent a 'six figure sum' to change the rotation of the Singapore Flyer observation wheel to improve its feng shui

➲ North Korea's vast Ryugyeong Hotel is still not finished – despite building work starting in 1987

❶ **Dancing Building, Prague, Czech Republic** Often nicknamed 'Drunk House', this building, built by Frank Gehry in 1996, was named after Fred Astaire and Ginger Rogers for its resemblance to a pair of dancers.

❷ **Beer Can House, Houston, Texas** John Milkovisch spent 18 years decorating his house with 39,000 beer cans, complete with 'can curtains' that chime in the wind.

❸ **Free Spirit House, British Columbia, Canada** Huge spherical wooden treehouses are suspended in the rainforest – visitors liken it to being 'adrift in a sea of trees and stars' or a 'magical pumpkin'.

❹ **Beer bottle temple, Sisaket, Thailand** Buddhist monks collected and recycled more than a million beer bottles to build the intricate Wat Pa Maha Chedi Kaew. We toast their hard work...

❺ **The Toilet, Seoul, South Korea** In a bid to lift the lid on poverty and poor sanitation, Sim Jae-duck built a house in the shape of a toilet – Haewoojae: 'a place of sanctuary where one can solve one's worries'. Donate $50,000 and a night on the loo can be yours.

❻ **Longaberger Basket, Newark, Ohio** The Longaberger Basket Company has stayed true to its passion and built its seven-storey HQ in the likeness of a woven basket, complete with huge metal handles.

❼ **Upside Down House, Syzmbark, Poland** This pad has been literally turned upside-down, designed by Daniel Czapiewski to remind people of wrongdoings against humanity.

❽ **The iPad, Dubai** This 23-storey tower, sitting in a 'docking station', is inspired by Apple's iPod.

❾ **Reversible density lofts, Tokyo, Japan** Floors are sloped, switches are hidden, cupboards are absent – architects Arakawa and Gins believe a stay "makes you alert and awakens instincts, so you'll live better, longer and even forever".

❿ **Piano House, Anhui, China** Enter through a delicate glass violin that leans against a beautiful black grand piano complete with white keys.

# }House of Weird

## Tales of architectural excess

**E**ver since the pharaohs decided some 5,000 years ago that a simple grave wasn't imposing enough, powerful men and women have resolved that bigger is better. The pursuit of might and mass has resulted in some incredible buildings – many created at enormous cost. But though the temples, pyramids and churches of history were monumental, recent technological advances have enabled the creation of some of the most extravagant buildings.

William Randolph Hearst, the great media magnate, set the bar high with his Cuesta Encantada ('Enchanted Hill'), or Hearst Castle, on California's central coast. Architect Julia Morgan based the original design on a Spanish cathedral but over nearly 30 years of construction it incorporated many styles – gothic, baroque, ancient Roman – and countless artifacts brought from Egypt, Morocco and

Europe. Not to mention tennis courts, a cinema, airfield, pools and the world's largest private zoo.

Dictators tend to share a love of decadence – witness Saddam Hussein's numerous, gilt-blinged palaces – but the biscuit was surely taken by Romanian tyrant Nicolae Ceauşescu. His vast Palace of the Parliament is an epic construction; the world's second-largest building, it cost US$3.3 billion, and around one-sixth of central Bucharest was bulldozed to make way for it. Started in 1984, its 24/7 construction was brought to a premature end by the 1989 revolution and the dictator's subsequent execution.

The title of World's Tallest Building is awarded and superseded so often it's hard to keep up. At the time of writing, Burj Dubai topped the list at around 820m – its architects won't confirm its final height, but since the previous incumbent was Taipei 101 at a 'mere' 509m, Burj Dubai is definitely top (until it's overtaken by the next one...)

## "The world's second-largest building cost $3.3 billion – one-sixth of Bucharest was bulldozed to make room"

**Top left:** "This church – in the tiny village of San Andrés Xecul, Guatemala – has to be the funkiest in all of Central America. Technicolour saints!"
*Seth Andersen*

**Top middle:** "One is not amused… the houses around Windsor Castle go wonky."
*Graham Berridge*

**Top right:** "This place is called *La maison du fou* – 'the house of the crackpot'."
*Fatma Girretz*

**Below left:** "This house is on an avenue of extravagant buildings built in the 1940s in the New Town of Quito, Ecuador, each trying to outdo its neighbours in the latest Art Deco or romantic style."
*Andrew Heppleston*

**Below right:** "This artist's house in Warburton, Victoria, Australia, is built out of wood and probably breaks every building rule."
*Markus Kaufmann*

**Above, top:** Housing blocks, Albanian style.
*Johnny Lawlor*

**Above, centre:** "Kyoto Railway Station, Japan, is truly spectacular, despite its facade being rather weird..."
*Marilyn Willwohl*

**Above:** Closed for business – "Walking around Johannesburg, we chanced upon this hotel, all bricked up at the entrance."
*Lau Pei Ling*

**Top right:** "A little down at heel... We saw this boot hotel in South Africa."
*Rachel Marchant*

**Below right:** "You can see the fetishes protecting this Tamberma house and its upstairs granaries in northern Togo – they keep it safe from enemy attack."
*Rhoda Allen*

**Above left & right:** "Just some of the bizarre buildings beside the Rhine in Dusseldorf, Germany."
*Steve Rudd*

**Left:** "Wildly over the top, but in the most impressive way – the Excalibur hotel and casino in Las Vegas."
*Joe Milton*

# }Big things

If you're cruising the roads near Kingston, South Australia, you might be forgiven for fearing an alien invasion as a vividly red, 17m-high lobster looms above. Calm yourself: 'Larry' is just one of around 150 'Big Things' to pop up Down Under in the past half-decade.

Initially built to highlight local agricultural sites, New South Wales' Big Banana was reputedly the first, in Coffs Harbour in 1964; the Big Pineapple followed in 1971 at Woombye, Queensland. Other big botanical and mycological marvels include apples, oranges, peanuts, mushrooms, avocados, cherries, potatoes, pumpkins, mangoes, strawberries, watermelons and – so very Aussie – a macadamia nut.

Animals play a big part: 'Rambo', Goulburn's Big Merino sheep (New South Wales) soars to 15m, while elsewhere you'll find chickens, prawns, crocs, crabs, cod and trout,

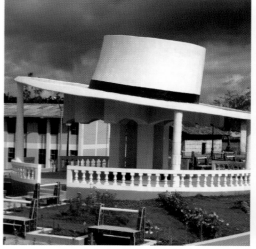

dogs, cows (and bulls), ants and mosquitoes, a penguin (at the small town of Penguin, Tasmania), whales and – naturally – kangaroos, koala and platypus. National heroes get a look in: you can meet a mighty Captain Cook, who charted Australia's coast, at Cairns; Ned Kelly dons his tin-bucket-helmet at Glenrowan, Victoria; and immigrants are celebrated with the Big Cornish Miner at Kapunda, and the Big Scotsman at Medindie, both South Australia.

Others showcase quintessentially Aussie obsessions: the Big Stubby – the typical beer bottle – at Tewantin, and the Big Pie at Yatala, both in Queensland.

And it's not just Australia that's awash with Big Things – visit giant sheep and dogs in New Zealand, pianos in China, guitars in Tennessee and the world's largest shelf of hardback books at the car park of Kentucky Public Library.

**"You might be forgiven for fearing an alien invasion as a vividly red, 17m-high lobster looms above"**

**Above:** "This giant prawn on Brighton seafront is supposed to entice people to the seafood shack next to it. But it looks more likely to eat you than be eaten *by* you."
*Jim Browning*

**Far left, top:** "The world's largest rocking horse lords over South Australia's Adelaide Hills."
*Sarah Baxter*

**Far left, centre:** "In the remote village of Celendin, in the highlands of Peru, the main village square consisted of, essentially, a hat."
*Dieter Turk*

**Far left, below:** A land of more sheep than people... "This corrugated tourist shop is near Whakatane, New Zealand."
*Ann Tubb*

**Centre left:** "A whole lot of fruit –Te Puke, New Zealand, is the world's kiwi capital."
*Sarah Baxter*

**Left:** "The Giant Crayfish's spindly legs loom over Kaikoura (meaning, funnily enough, crayfish meal), New Zealand."
*Sarah Baxter*

# Art of darkness

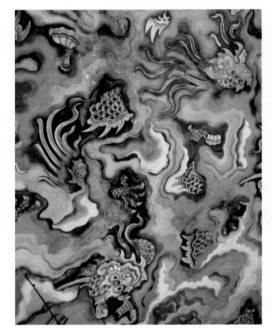

**Top left:** "This painting adorns the ceiling of an emperor's tomb in Hué, Vietnam. The story goes that the artist painted it with his feet."
*Ruth Kennedy*

**Top right:** "At the 'merry cemetery' in Sapinta, Romania, gravestones each contain a 'wee me' by which to remember the deceased."
*Kris Weber*

**Right:** "This was taken in central Prague, among throngs of tourists – none of whom had noticed this hanging iron figure."
*Peter Bemmer*

**Far right:** "These 'Hands of Hell' at the White Temple, Chiang Rai, Thailand, symbolise those wanting to escape the pit of hell and enter the gates of heaven."
*Sandra Bell & Nathan Fender*

# Bones of an idea

There are many spots where morbid travellers can wander among human remains – catacombs in Paris and Rome, vast cemeteries and necropolises such as Highgate's gothic marvels in London, and tombs like the Pyramids. But for artistic extravagance, the ossuary of Sedlec at Kutná Hora in the Czech Republic is unrivalled.

The town's Cistercian monastery became a popular resting place in the 13th century after Abbot Henry sprinkled the cemetery with earth from the Holy Land – so much so that they ran out of space, and bones had to be piled up in the small All Saints' chapel.

In 1870 the woodcarver František Rint was commissioned by the land's owners, the Schwarzenberg family, to make something special from the bones. And he really let rip, creating crosses, monstrances, bells, the Schwarzenberg coat of arms and a huge chandelier incorporating every bone of the human body.

The ossuary is open daily, and easily accessible on a day trip from Prague, 65km to the north-west.

**Top & below left & centre:** "In the Sedlec Ossuary thousands of bones are artistically arranged to form decorations and furnishings, complete with a coat of arms and goblet constructed from bones."
*Natalie Finlayson*

**Below right:** "The interior of Sedlec is constructed from the bones of some 40,000 human skeletons. "
*Jonathan Lopez*

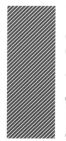

**G**raffiti: art or vandalism? Discuss...

The modern word is derived from the Italian word *graffiato*, meaning scratched. The first known example of graffiti was discovered in the ancient city of Ephesus (modern-day Efes, Turkey): a footprint, a number and a handprint that closely resembles a heart etched in stone – purportedly an advert for a brothel, the hand symbolising payment.

Other ancient graffiti can be found preserved at Pompeii, Italy – caricatures of politicians, Latin curses, declarations of love and the boastful: '*Suspirium puellarum Celadus thraex*' – 'Celadus the Thracian makes the girls moan'!

The Vikings left similarly saucy marks on the Neolithic burial mound at Maes Howe in the Orkneys, Scotland; when the tomb was excavated in 1861, archaeologists uncovered walls scratched with 12th-century Viking texts, including: 'Thorni bedded, Helgi carved.'

Romeo and Juliet fans flock from to write love notes on the walls of Casa di Giulietta in Verona, Italy. A wall made of removable panels is now regarded as a real work of popular art and the town is considering a museum to house the previously removed panels of graffiti.

A famous graffiti artist's inscription can be found at the Temple of Poseidon in Attica, Greece. Now framed, 'Byron' is the inscription, presumed to be Britain's very own Lord Byron.

Elsewhere, if you desperately want to partake in some vandalism, don't do it at the Great Wall of China. To combat graffiti a bogus wall of marble bricks has been built near the most-visited section of the wall. Visitors are fooled/encouraged to carve their sentiments on a brick for the sum of $120.

The power of graffiti was confirmed when *Space Girl & Bird*, a work by 'guerrilla artist' Banksy, sold at auction for £288,000 in 2007. And it was reported in 2008 that the value of a derelict Liverpool pub had been doubled by the addition of a Banksy mural – of a giant rat...

> **"Ancient graffiti at Pompeii included caricatures of politicians, curses and sexual boasts"**

**Top far left:** "I spotted this dilemma near the cathedral in Granada, Spain: should you go left for the good of your soul or right for more physical activities?"
*Peter Ashton*

**Below far left:** Crime scene or art attack? Bilbao, Spain.
*David Fernandez*

**Below left:** "We'd been out walking around the centre of Prague, Czech Republic, and found this graffiti down a backstreet. It seemed such a shame that it was hidden away out of view."
*Lindsay Fane*

**Left:** "Ummmmm... Not for children's eyes – art at London's Tate Modern."
*Chris Mole*

**Far left, top:** "This painting on a house in Québec City, Canada, looks almost real. It tells stories from its past to visitors, who can enjoy a free history class looking at this piece of art."
*Marilyn Champagne*

**Far left, centre:** "At the parking area for New Zealand's Fox Glacier we came upon this van. The insurance has been taken care of – instructions are clear!"
*Carlota Godinho*

**Far left, below:** "After enjoying the beautiful autumn leaves in Luleå, northern Sweden, we had a quick look around the rather deserted town and I spotted this sad cloud on a wall."
*Sophie Atkinson*

**Top left:** "Squat in Berlin, Germany, 1975; anarchists had taken over derelict buildings and created their own mini-village and artworks."
*Chris Prior*

**Below left:** Grim graffiti coats the seafront in Split, Croatia.
*Steve Rudd*

**Top right:** "I stumbled upon this graffitied hedge behind the Musées royaux des Beaux-Arts in Brussels, Belgium – an alternative to the art on display inside, perhaps?"
*Eileen Strong*

**Right:** "Who wants to see out of a window anyway? This quirky artwork was created on a window in the old town of Ljubljana, Slovenia."
*Steve Morgan*

**Far right, centre:** It's not just a man thing – "This photo was taken inside the ladies' toilets at a late-night café in Sydney, Australia."
*Louise Mortimer*

**Far right, below:** "My son tried on this clog in Amsterdam, Netherlands."
*Ron Toothill*

# )Dessication creations

Death Valley is a spooky enough place at the best of times: arid, shimmering in the incredible heat, and largely empty save some snakes and a few hardy bighorn sheep. The surrounding area is equally mind-bending, encompassing a former atomic test site, an isolated opera house and some hot springs. Stop at Rhyolite, a ghost town at the desert's north-east edge, and you'll find some surprises – not least the Goldwell Open Air Museum. Conceived as a sculpture garden by Belgian artist Albert Szulalski, his sombre white figures have been joined by an array of alternative art – look out for a rainbow-hued mosaic sofa *(far right)* and the pixellated 'Lady Desert' *(above)*.

In Chile's Atacama Desert a huge hand stretches out from the sand south of Antofagasta: Mario Irarrázaval's *mano del desierto (opposite, right)*, sculpted from granite in 1992. And in the USA, 38 cars were hefted into place in 1987 to create 'Carhenge' *(left and above left)* in Nebraska.

**Far left, top & below:** "Welcome to Carhenge (Alliance, Nebraska), a stacked-up, welded-together collection of old bangers replicating an ancient wonder."
*Joseph Brennan*

**Opposite, top:** "Desert Barbie!"
*Ben Moulam*

**Above:** "In the middle of the desert in Chile a buried giant is trying to escape!"
*Ben Moulam*

**Far left, below:** "Cadillac Ranch is a public art installation and sculpture in a cow pasture on the edge of Amarillo, Texas."
*Deborah Erwin*

**Left:** "Sitting comfortably in Death Valley, California."
*Ben Moulam*

# Statuesque style

**Above left:** "I found these intriguing moss-covered stone heads in the back garden of a merchant's town house in Amsterdam, Netherlands. I've no idea what they are for."
*Lesley Heptinstall*

**Far left, below:** Giants parade the streets during the Fiesta de la Santísima Cruz de Caravaca, Murcia, Spain.
*Paul Morrison*

**Below left:** A new meaning to breastfeeding in the Piazza Duomo, Amalfi, Italy.
*Tom Charnock*

**Above:** "Some strange sculptures have been installed in front of the Dubai International Financial Centre ('The Gate'). These ants are digging into a grassy roundabout; they are oversized and even have eggs trailing behind them."
*Christine Theodorovics*

**Top left:** "Hmmm… not sure what is going on here. The 'City of Ghosts', in Sichuan Province, China, is one of the most bizarre places I've ever been, with statues of very strange goings-on! To be honest, the entire city could be in this book."
*Chris Hopkinson*

**Top middle:** "In India, even Jesus needs protection from Kerala's sun and monsoons!"
*Anne Siller*

**Top right:** Bovine boogie – "Part of the Cow Parade event in San José, Costa Rica."
*Lucy Jefferys*

**Right:** "A hot day's shopping in Adelaide, Australia, and I was making a pig of myself with an ice lolly. I trotted off to look for a bin for my wrapper, but did a double take when I saw these porkers."
*Ian Forder*

**Top left:** "This intimate statue is stuck on the front of St Domnius Cathedral in Split, Croatia."
*Tom Charnock*

**Top middle:** "It was gala night in the ship's restaurant – this 'sculpture' is made of white chocolate!"
*Alan King*

**Top right:** "All the gargoyles on the Basílica del Voto Nacional in Quito, Ecuador, are native animals and birds, from crocodiles to jaguars. These birds were 'perched' precariously, appearing ready to dive bomb any unsuspecting sinners."
*Andrew Heppleston*

**Left:** "Along the riverbanks of Singapore, members of an artistic family sit on a bench, waiting for admirers to take their photos."
*Champaklal Lad*

# Keeping it surreal

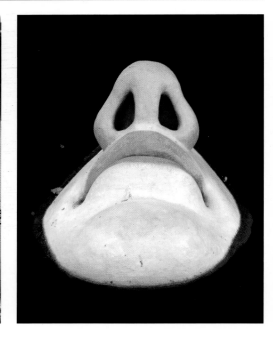

## SALVADOR DALÍ: art's eccentric auteur

**K**nown for his famously eccentric work – melting clocks, lobster telephones, elephants on stilts – the life of Salvador Dalí (1904-1989) echoed his surreal art. Born in Catalunya, Spain, Dalí was precociously talented, first exhibiting his work aged 14, going on to produce what he called 'hand-painted dream photographs'.

To get a better feel for the overlap between reality and surreality, explore Catalunya's 'Dalí triangle'. First up, visit the Teatre-Museu Dalí in his birthplace, Figueres. The first clue to the surprises and illusions lurking within is the array of eggs perched on the top. At the centre of the Mae West room is a sofa in the shape of a voluptuous pair of lips; viewed from the entrance, the room transforms into the face of the sensual actress.

In 1968 Dalí bought a medieval keep, Castell de Pubol, for his wife, Gala. His notoriously promiscuous spouse is said to have sent for young village men while in residence almost until her death at age 88; her husband, meanwhile, was required to apply (in writing) for permission to attend. Dalí renovated the castle in typically bizarre style: Gala's final resting place here is guarded by a stuffed giraffe.

The final point of the triangle is Dalí's home, Casa Museu Salvador Dalí in the fishing village of Port Lligat. Built over the course of his life, the house has become a winding maze with narrow corridors that open into rooms packed with mementoes of his life and (rather odd) work. Dalí described it as "like a true biological structure ... Each new pulse in our life has its own new cell, a room."

 **"In typically bizarre style, the final resting place of Dalí's wife, Gala, is guarded by a stuffed giraffe"**

**Opposite, far left:** "In Christchurch, New Zealand, there is a Mini Cooper mounted on a wall, complete with parking sign!"
*Lauren Laman*

**Opposite, centre:** Though the swinging 60s are long gone, San Francisco's Haight-Ashbury area is still true to its bohemian roots.
*Robert Child*

**Opposite, right:** "Art lurking in the Medici Fountain, Paris."
*Donal O'Leary*

**Above left:** "I took this in Brienz, Switzerland – something wacky in well-ordered Switzerland!"
*Robert Child*

**Above right:** "I never saw anyone try to sit at this table in Liotta village, Lesbos, Greece, but after an ouzo or two, anything is possible."
*Roy Lawrance*

**This page, far left:** The Beer Chandelier – "A lot of work went into producing the empties for this magnificent masterpiece, located at Planet Baobab camping ground, Botswana."
*Anthony Bianco*

**Left:** "Crayola rules in Bremen, Germany. This is the monument for those unhappy kids whose drawings, no matter what they intended to represent, always came up as blobby hippopotamuses."
*Dariusz Jankowski*

**Top far left:** "This bench sits outside the Modern Art Museum in Stockholm, Sweden."
*Hayley Dunning*

**Top left:** Just enjoying the moo-sic at Herefordshire's Big Chill Festival, UK.
*Maria Galvin*

**Centre, far left:** "Wax statues are put up all over Valencia, Spain, for Las Fallas festival, and burned on the last night."
*Rob Langford*

**Centre left:** Albania's once-grey beach bunkers are now curiously colourful.
*Paul Morrison*

**Below far left:** Would you like a bag for that? "This plastic camel (why would you need a plastic camel?) was half wrapped and stood in Aït Benhaddou, Morocco."
*Kiki Streitberger*

**Below left:** "This penguin was in a doorway in the Italian city of Orvieto, better known for its buildings than its fake birds!"
*Lesley Heptinstall*

**Right, top to bottom:** "These figures in Dongyue Temple, Beijing, China, depict elements of the Taoist supernatural world."
*Marie Timmermans*

**Top right:** "A spaceship from the movie *Pitch Black* was left in Coober Pedy, South Australia, after filming. This subterranean town must be the only spot where a spaceship doesn't look out of place."
*Sophie Collard*

**Right:** A cow in a tree, – Melbourne, Australia.
*Penny Clark*

**Far right, centre:** "This panda is doing his thing on Beijing's Tiananmen Square, China."
*Richard Asher*

**Far right, below:** "I found this oversized vegetable garden 'growing' in the Cameron Highlands, Malaysia."
*Samantha Dobson*

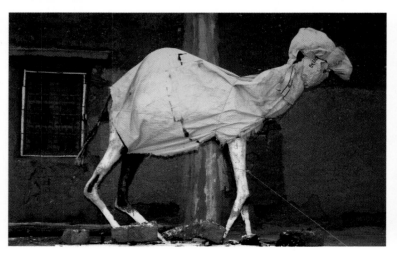

# )Signs: uh, what?

ON THIS SPOT IN 1765 NOTHING HAPPENED

MEDICINE NO FAKES

Castaways →

ตัวมอม
MOM

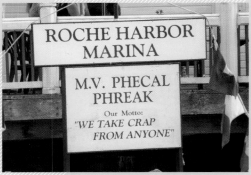
ROCHE HARBOR MARINA

M.V. PHECAL PHREAK

Our Motto:
"WE TAKE CRAP FROM ANYONE"

THIS CAFE IS RELUCTANTLY OFFERED FOR SALE DUE TO WIFE NOT TAKING THE PILL

PILES

Welcome to OODNADATTA

HORSE

THE AUSTRALIAN
FEARS FOR MISSING DIGGERS

Townsville BULLETIN
MISSING DIGGERS FOUND

Courier-M
STOP BLACK DOL

for dogs and... camels only!

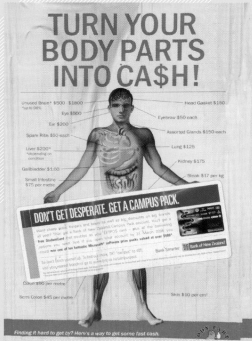

TURN YOUR BODY PARTS INTO CA$H!

THICKLY SETTLED

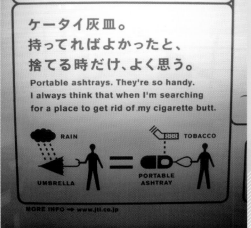

ケータイ灰皿。
持ってればよかったと、
捨てる時だけ、よく思う。

Portable ashtrays. They're so handy. I always think that when I'm searching for a place to get rid of my cigarette butt.

MORE INFO ➔ www.jti.co.jp

COLON FLUID

Pod slap

LONG RANGE WEATHER FORECAST HOT HOT AND DAMNED HOT
LAST RAIN
LAST SNOW-THE ICE AGE

UPSTEPS TO SUNKEN GARDEN

GLEN CLOSE

Esther Gellings; Andy Henius; Garry Ho; Anastasiya Govodilova; Terry Dormer; Barry O'Sullivan; Samantha Dobson; Graham Keetch; Andrew Swaffer; Kris Weber; Ingrid Morgan; Maren Hills; Becky Hemsley; Nikoleta Simunekova; Ann Tubb; Nigel Drury; Rob Hawthorne; Sue Hirst

# Indescribably
# strange

**So weird we don't know what to call them – this array
of mummies, mailboxes and more beggars belief**

**Double-barrel bunny:** "Armed and ready for action, this bunny guards an ATM on the island of Patmos, Greece."
*Lisa Burns*

# It's a **hoax, folks!**

In 1912, Charles Dawson announced the discovery in Sussex of a remarkable palaeontological find: fragments of a skull and jawbone that seemed to be from an early human. Dated to some 500,000 years ago, the discovery caused an uproar; the remains of 'Piltdown Man' were feted as a 'missing link'.

It wasn't until 1953 that further analysis showed the skull was human, from the medieval period, while the jaw – from an orang-utan – was 500 years old; both had been stained to indicate great age. In short, it was a hoax – but one which fooled many of the great minds of the day, and which remains one of the most famous spoofs of all time.

Of course, in some situations it's called fraud, while on other occasions such fakes are applauded by those suckered as well as the perpetrators – the British TV news programme *Panorama*'s 1960s broadcast showing spaghetti trees being harvested is cherished as a classic.

Elsewhere, crop circles, alien sightings and the Loch Ness Monster are all perennial favourites. And some historic hoaxes continue to fascinate long after they've been debunked.

For example, in 1726, Mary Tofts convinced several doctors that she'd given birth to multiple rabbits; indeed, she proceeded to 'deliver' dead rabbits in the presence of two of Britain's leading doctors. In 1770, Wolfgang von Kempelen presented a miraculous 'chess automaton', The Turk, to the Austrian court. This mechanical marvel defeated a number of top chess players, and toured Europe for more than 50 years before being exposed as a hoax, containing a person who directed the moves. In 1917 two young girls, Elsie Wright and Frances Griffiths, presented the first of a series of photos showing groups of fairies cavorting with them. Sir Arthur Conan Doyle, creator of Sherlock Holmes and an ardent spiritualist, was persuaded to support them, and the girls didn't admit the hoax until the 1980s.

And, of course, for serious conspiracy theorists there's always the moon landings…

**Opposite:** "The morning after my first night at Oktoberfest, I thought a nice stroll around Olympic Park might clear my head. Then I came across this. Maybe Munich's park designers enjoyed Oktoberfest a tad too much as well… and suddenly, I didn't half fancy a kickabout!"
*Darren Lee*

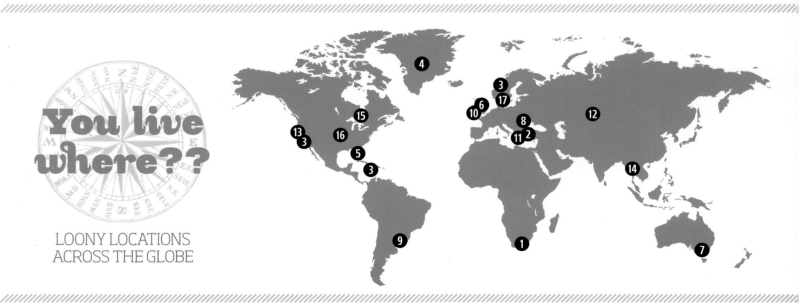

## You live where??

### LOONY LOCATIONS ACROSS THE GLOBE

**❶ Tweebuffelsmeteenskoot-morsdoodgeskietfontein, South Africa** 'Two buffaloes shot dead using one shot fountain' sounds more fun in Afrikaans.

**❷ Batman, south-east Turkey** A real-life Gotham, with oil rigs.

**❸ Hell** You *can* find Hell on earth – in spots ranging from California to the Cayman Islands to Norway.

**❹ Hold With Hope, Greenland** Remain optimistic among the wolves and muskoxen of the Arctic.

**❺ Mianus, Florida** It's not yours, it's mine...

**❻ Lickey End, UK** While away your time in the West Midlands.

**❼ Tittybong, Australia** Titter in this tiny town in north-west Victoria.

**❽ Turda, Romania** This scatologically-titled town has been around for 2,000 years.

**❾ Morón, Argentina** You'd be daft not to visit the town's Cathedral of Nuestra Señora del Buen Viaje.

**❿ Brown Willy, UK** Hike up the highest point in Cornwall.

**⓫ Puke, Albania** But the locals pronounce it 'Pooka'.

**⓬ Nuke, Kazakhstan** Have a blast in the country's east.

**⓭ Zzyzx, California** Officially the world's alphabetically last place name.

**⓮ Krung Thep Mahanakhon Amon Rattanakosin Mahinthara Ayuthaya Mahadilok Phop Noppharat** Ratchathani Burirom Udomratchaniwet Mahasathan Amon Piman Awatan Sathit Sakkathattiya Witsanukam Prasit, Thailand And breathe... The official title of Thai capital Bangkok.

**⓯ Punkeydoodles Corners, Canada** Less place, more bend in the road with an oft-stolen sign.

**⓰ Nameless, Tennessee** So good they named it nonce.

**⓱ Middelfart, Denmark** Childish, yes; funny, YES!

**Right:** "A skeleton kicks back at the Natural History Museum of Sydney, Australia."
*Christelle Royet*

**Top right:** "The soil of Guanajuato, north-west of Mexico City, favours preservation of corpses – so much so that the city has opened a rather odd museum displaying some of the many mummies that have been found in the area. This is perhaps the highlight: the smallest mummy in the world."
*Gregory Froome*

**Opposite, bottom left:** "Corn bath, California, USA."
*Sarah Davis-Goff*

**Opposite, bottom centre:** Truly hot mail, in the hills outside Melbourne, Australia: "I often wonder if the post is burnt when the owner picks it up in the morning..."
*Heather Macmillan*

**Opposite, bottom right:** "Some of the antics people get up to at festivals, in this case the Big Chill, UK – glitter wrestling?!"
*Maria Galvin*

# CHARMING EMBALMING:
## the mummy story

**F**orget Boris Karloff, Brendan Fraser and Hammer horror films – the real processes behind those bandage-swathed bogeymen were much more stomach-churning than anything in the movies.

Well before ancient Egyptians ensured their entrance into the afterlife with embalming – from as early as 5,000BC – the Chinchorro culture of present-day Peru and Chile practised mummification. Unlike in Egypt, everyone was mummified – including foetuses. Early mummification utilised the 'black technique': the body was disassembled and heat-dried, then reassembled and covered with white ash paint before the skin was re-attached and painted with manganese. The 'red technique' was introduced around 3,000BC: all organs were removed – the head cut off to remove the brain – and replaced with materials such as hair, before the body was painted with red ochre.

The removal of soft organs is vital for successful embalming. The Egyptians didn't remove the head, instead pulling the brain out through the nose with a hook. They used salt to dry the body before wrapping it in flaxen cloth and gum.

But mummification is not just the, er, preserve of the ancients; 20th-century communists took a shine to it, too. Perhaps inspired by the discovery of Tutankhamun's tomb in 1922, Lenin was embalmed after his death in 1924. And successfully so – his waxy body is on display to this day in Moscow (though every now and then he has to be removed for a chemical re-dipping – recipe: a Russian secret).

Subsequently Mao Zedong, Ho Chi Minh and North Korean leader Kim Il Sung have all been mummified, and are all laid out for public perusal – a ghoulish gateway into world history.

> ## "The Egyptians didn't remove the head, instead pulling the brain out through the nose with a hook"

**Above:** Now, this is mountain biking… "The assembly of a bike we were using for medical research into altitude illness in the Hidden Valley in the Dhaulagiri region, Nepal."
*Zoe Smith*

**Right:** "A French dog from Russia, wearing a hat fashioned by his owner, at the yacht club in Kalkan, Turkey."
*Gizelle Gill*

**Far right, centre:** "I stumbled across these 'love letters' pasted onto a disused factory building in a backstreet in Auckland, New Zealand. There was no explanation that I could see."
*Mel Head*

**Far right, below:** "A really pants photo at a campsite in France."
*Sue Whiskin*

# TRUE STORIES: belting out a Borneo karaoke

"There are two ways into Gunung Mulu National Park: by river or by air. Our journey began on a Twin Otter propeller plane, which proudly displayed the smart red-and-blue livery of Malaysia Airlines on the outside, and 14 metal car seats bolted to the floor on the inside. A marginally more upholstered longboat took us upriver, into the heart of Borneo.

It had taken days to reach Rumah Bala Lasong, a traditional Iban longhouse in Gunung Mulu's midst. Tramping through a thick mass of creeper vines, bamboo and fig trees, we arrived shortly before nightfall. Housing 28 families, several hundred geckos, several thousand mosquitoes, five mongrels, numerous chickens and – for tonight – at least one rather apprehensive traveller, the longhouse was a ramshackle wooden construction built on stilts, with a corrugated tin roof that turned the place into an oven when the equatorial sun beat down on it.

The Iban people had no fridge, no flush toilets, no telephone, and our beds for the night were hand-woven bamboo mats set upon the bare splintered floorboards of the vast communal living room.

It therefore came as something of a surprise when Bala Lasong, the longhouse chief, appeared in a tribal headdress and an Adidas tracksuit, wheeling in a new karaoke machine.

"Rice wine?" he asked, and decanted a cloudy liquid from a petrol can into plastic beakers. As Bala Lasong continued to ply us with rice wine, and the longhouse rang to the sound of drunken renditions of 'I Will Survive', I reflected that this wasn't quite what I had expected to find in the heart of Borneo."
*Professor Yaffle, on www.goWander.com*

**Above, left:** "The 'Lavatree' in Australia."
*Michelle Rive*

**Above, centre:** "A mailbox with a difference in Hurunui, South Island, New Zealand."
*Lyn Hughes*

**Above, right:** "A 'Pustefix' bear blowing bubbles in Utrecht, Netherlands."
*Bernhard Bachner*

PUSSY WILLOW

**Far left & left:** "Eager drinker in Lillehammer, Norway."
*Joanne Fletcher*

**Far left, below:** "Pussy willow, Australian style!"
*Andrew Swaffer*

**Below left:** "On the road between El Calafate and El Chaltén in Patagonia is a small café and hostel where the buses stop for refreshments. Perched in a tree outside I spotted this rather macabre dead dog's head."
*Sophie Atkinson*

**Right:** "These telly addicts were spotted boating through the early morning mists on the Ganges, India."
*Josie Budd*

**Below:** "This phone and its shelter were located along a quiet road in Oban, Stewart Island, New Zealand."
*Ann Tubb*

**Below, centre:** For trunk calls? Staying connected in NZ.
*Paul Morrison*

**Below, right:** "This shopping centre in Delhi features a very odd entrance: 'Piccadelhi' phoneboxes give an unexpected taste of London."
*Chloe Govan*

# Bradt

For more than 35 years Bradt has been helping adventurous travellers to reach some of the weirdest - and most wonderful - parts of the world. Our motto has always been 'Take the Road Less Travelled' and not only do we take pride in pioneering unusual destinations, we also delight in all that is quirky and different. With over 130 titles to choose from, plus a range of illustrated wildlife guides, many of our books are unique.

Looking for travel with a difference? You can count on Bradt to provide insight, inspiration and independent information.

www.bradtguides.com

# Wanderlust

If you want to get off the beaten track and roam this weird world of ours, you need *Wanderlust*.

*Wanderlust* is the magazine for people who love to get out there and explore – travellers who long to escape the crowds and seek out the most unique cultures, wildlife and activities. Since 1993 we've been providing the inspiration and information to help people like you discover the most authentic experiences all over the planet.

So before you plan your next big adventure, make sure you take a journey with *Wanderlust*.

**www.wanderlust.co.uk**